RIO GRANDE CIVIL WAR TRAIL

MAP LEGEND/LEYENDA

 CITY - *Cuidad*

 RANCH - *Rancho*

 MUSEUM - *Museo*

 BATTLE - *Batalla*

 CEMETERY/GRAVE - *Cementerio/Sepultura*

 LIGHTHOUSE - *Faro*

 CAMP - *Campamento*

 FORT - *Fuerte*

 HOUSE/HOSPITAL - *Casa/Hospital*

 STEAMBOAT - *Vapor*

 PLAZA - *Plaza*

 BRIDGE - *Puente*

 Follow this link to the Rio Grande Valley Civil War Trail. Under "Quick Links" click on Tourism Brochure/Map to order the full-size official map.

Blue and Gray
on the Border

Publication of this book was supported
by a gift from the Texas Historical Foundation.

A&M travel guides

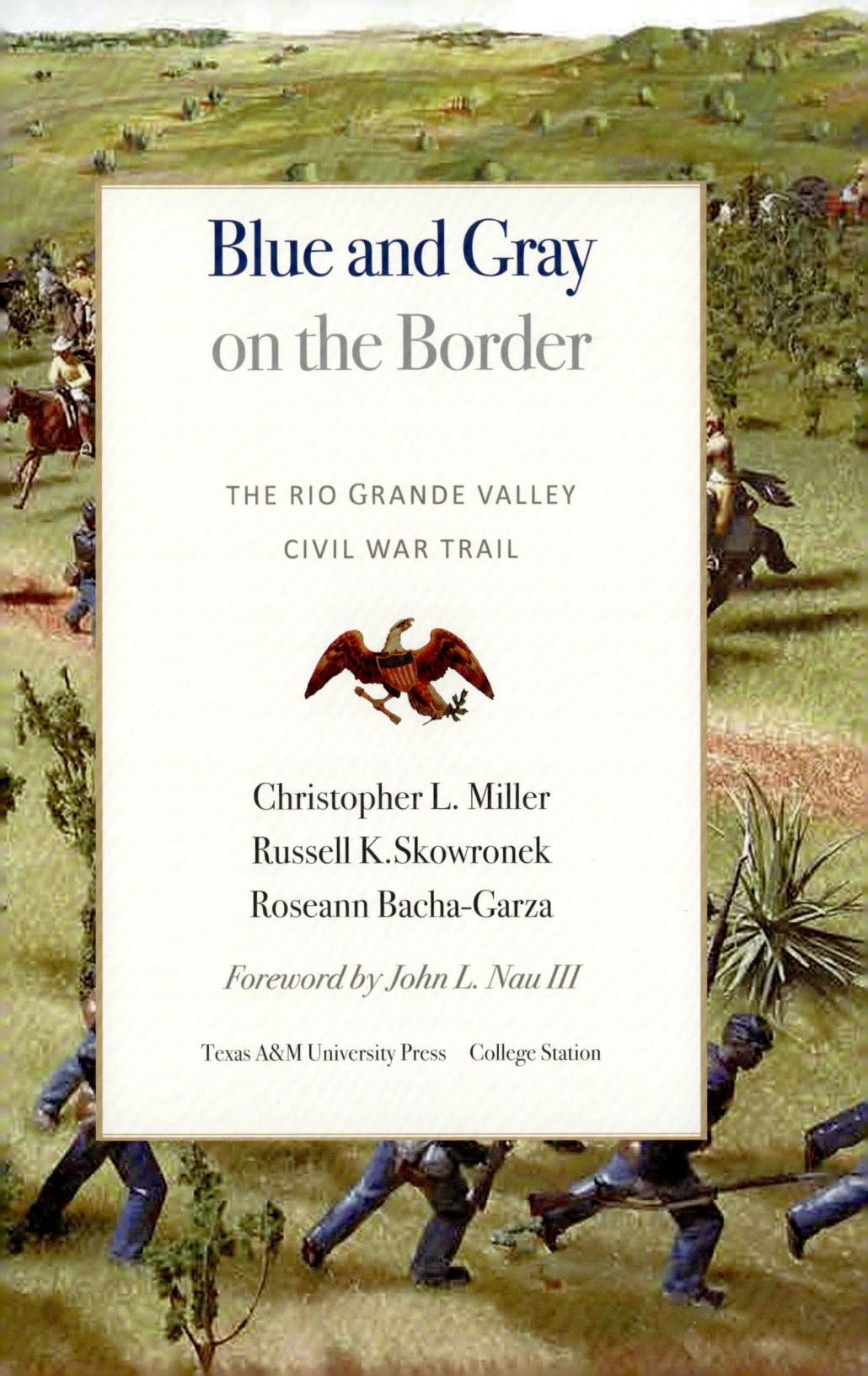

Blue and Gray on the Border

THE RIO GRANDE VALLEY CIVIL WAR TRAIL

Christopher L. Miller
Russell K. Skowronek
Roseann Bacha-Garza

Foreword by John L. Nau III

Texas A&M University Press   College Station

Copyright © 2018
Christopher L. Miller,
Russell K. Skowronek,
and Roseann Bacha-Garza
All rights reserved
First edition

This paper meets the requirements
of ANSI/NISO Z39.48-1992 (Permanence of Paper).
Binding materials have been chosen for durability.
Manufactured in China through Four Colour Print Group.

Library of Congress Cataloging-in-Publication Data

Names: Miller, Christopher L., 1950– author. | Skowronek, Russell K., author. | Bacha-Garza, Roseann, author.
Title: Blue and gray on the border : the Rio Grande Valley Civil War trail / Christopher L. Miller, Russell K. Skowronek, Roseann Bacha-Garza ; foreword by John L. Nau III.
Description: First edition. | College Station : Texas A&M University Press, [2018] | Includes index.
Identifiers: LCCN 2018007912 | ISBN 9781623496821 (book/flexbound (with flaps) : alk. paper) | ISBN 9781623496845 (e-book)
Subjects: LCSH: Lower Rio Grande Valley (Tex.)--History, Military--19th century. | Texas--History--Civil War, 1861-1865--Guidebooks. | Historic sites--Texas--Lower Rio Grande Valley--Guidebooks. | Military archaeology--Texas--Lower Rio Grande Valley--Guidebooks. | Lower Rio Grande Valley (Tex.)--Guidebooks. | LCGFT: Guidebooks.
Classification: LCC F392.R5 M56 2018 | DDC 976.4/05--dc23 LC record available at https://lccn.loc.gov/2018007912

Front cover courtesy of Texas Civil War Museum, Fort Worth, Texas.
Back cover: Port Isabel Lighthouse courtesy of Museums of Port Isabel. Map courtesy of the Texas General Land Office (map #93903).
Sketch of US barracks destroyed at Fort Brown by C. E. H. Bonwill, 1864.

Dedicated to Karen G. Fort, Tom A. Fort, Rolando Garza, James N. Leiker, Irving W. Levinson, Mary Margaret McAllen, W. Stephen McBride, Douglas A. Murphy, and Jerry D. Thompson, whose expertise formed the foundation of the Rio Grande Valley Civil War Trail. Their scholarly input has provided a pool of knowledge from which we have drawn while molding this book.

Dedicated also to Samantha Bernard, who, it is fair to say, "blazed the trail" in her 2012 exploration of the Laredo–Brownsville route. She is the future of historical archaeology.

Contents

Foreword, by John L. Nau III ix
Preface: Born of Frustration: Building the
    Rio Grande Valley Civil War Trail xiii
Acknowledgments xxi
Introduction: How to Use This Book 1

1. The Contested History of the Rio Grande Valley:
   Framing the Civil War Era 3
2. Cameron County Sites and Events 33
3. Hidalgo County Sites and Events 79
4. Starr County Sites and Events 103
5. Zapata County Sites and Events 129
6. Webb County Sites and Events 143
7. US Colored Troops 162
8. Beyond the Rio Grande Valley Civil War Trail:
   Exploring the American Civil War in
   Texas and Mexico 174

Epilogue 189
About the Authors 193
Index 195

Foreword

In July 2016, I presented the Rio Grande Valley Civil War Trail project with the Texas Historical Commission's Chairman's Award for Community Education. At that time, I praised the project as "a robust education initiative that reaches audiences from school children to tourists visiting the region." Then as now, I was impressed with the bilingual guide that takes tourists through a five-county region and the accompanying website that shares additional information and stories about this pivotal period in our history.

This new book moves the project forward in important ways. It not only builds on the project's research, but it also expands the printed guide and digital website into an illustrated format accessible to both heritage tourists on the road and armchair tourists reading at home. And, it will become an invaluable educational tool for students who want to know more about the history of this region.

When it comes to Civil War history, the Rio Grande Valley is often overlooked. Major battles and campaigns of the Eastern and Western Theater, such as Gettysburg, Antietam, Vicksburg, and Sherman's March to the Sea, are often discussed in high school classes. Texas students are often told of John Bell Hood and the Battles of Galveston and Sabine Pass; however, the importance of the Rio Grande Valley to the Confederate economy or of the troop buildup along the Texas-Mexico border is rarely addressed. If anything, Texas students are sometimes taught the trivia tidbit that the last battle of the war (Palmito Ranch) took place in Texas a month after Robert E. Lee surrendered at Appomattox Court House and that it was a Confederate victory. But students are not always taught that this battle took place in the Valley. Nor are they taught anything substantial about the battle, let alone the Valley's role in the Civil War more broadly.

This book highlights two themes that are often underplayed in histories of the Confederacy but are crucial to our understanding of the history of both the Civil War and Texas—the importance of the international cotton trade through Mexico and the racial, ethnic, and cultural diversity of the region.

As the Union blockade off the Confederate coastline increasingly limited shipping from ports along the Gulf of Mexico and the Atlantic Ocean, trade with Mexico at river ports along the Rio Grande became a critical lifeline for the Confederate economy, which depended heavily on exports of cotton to Europe, and for the Confederacy's ability to import both military supplies as well as the basic necessities of day-to-day life for civilians. Cotton from Texas, Louisiana, and Arkansas arrived in Brownsville and was transported across the river to Matamoros before being taken to the Mexican port of Bagdad, where ships from around the world waited. By 1863, this was the only effective international shipping point in the South, and President Abraham Lincoln and Union leaders wanted it shut down. As a force of seven thousand Union troops arrived near Brownsville on November 2, 1863, Confederate forces decided to evacuate Brownsville and nearby Fort Brown, burning their supplies and cotton as they fled. Union soldiers then marched into the city unopposed on the morning of November 6. The bustling cotton trade shifted upriver to Laredo and Eagle Pass, but returned to Brownsville in 1864 when Confederates regained control of the city.

In addition to the underappreciated economic role of the Valley, also too often ignored is the social history of the Valley during the war. When Texas seceded from the United States in 1861, the Rio Grande Valley was already a diverse community of Mexicans, naturalized Tejanos, Anglo Texans, European immigrants, mixed-race families, and freedmen. Enslaved persons were not commonly found in the region, but slavery did exist on a small scale. In addition, runaway slaves often traversed the Valley as they sought refuge across the Rio Grande in Mexico. When Union troops arrived in Texas in 1863, the region's ethnic diversity changed yet again. Among the ranks of the Union forces were not only white soldiers and officers but thousands of African Americans who were members of US Colored Troops regiments. After the end of the war and throughout the Reconstruction Era, regiments consisting of African American soldiers continued to patrol the border and maintain peace on the frontier. In many ways, I see this Civil War era community as a microcosm of the future United States and its place in the global economy.

Although the name of the trail and this book emphasize the Civil War, this book and its trail sites are by no means limited to the 1861–65 timeframe. The book and trail also focus on significant historical sites that are important markers of pre–Civil War events dating back to the Mexican War. The inclusion of these sites is an important contribution to the historiography of the region and heritage tourism in the Valley. The Mexican War sites on the trail and what happened at these places during the period between the signing of the Treaty of Guadalupe Hidalgo in 1848 and the firing of the first shots at Fort Sumter in April 1861 set the stage for what was to come during the Civil War. Without their inclusion, readers would have a far less complete understanding of the history of the Rio Grande Valley and its vital role during the Civil War. The authors' inclusion of these sites in the book make it all the more indispensable to heritage tourists wanting to experience the history of this place and others who wish to have a richer understanding of the history of Texas.

In short, this book brings important attention to this region and its significance in not just the Civil War but American history more generally. By connecting events and people with specific places, historic sites, and markers, the book does something that has not been done before—it takes readers on a tour of a five-county region and places the Valley in the broader context of American history. It is my hope, and the hope of the authors, that this book will not only increase awareness of the Rio Grande region, but also encourage and inspire readers to travel here and explore and study these sites for themselves.

John L. Nau III
Houston, Texas
October 25, 2017

Preface

Born of Frustration: Building the Rio Grande Valley Civil War Trail

Sometimes good ideas are born out of frustration.[1] Early in the spring of 2012, we were chatting about the promise of public history in the Rio Grande Valley in a darkened office on the campus of what was then the University of Texas–Pan American (UTPA). As will often transpire in such discussions, there was a lament over how events elsewhere in the country have really marginalized our local history, giving it a less than savory character. We discussed the significant role of the region in the history of the United State from the Mexican-American War, which led to the annexation of a vast portion of Mexico, to John Pershing and the run-up to WWI, and the continued presence of US Army troops along the international border until 1944. How to capitalize on these incidents was the question. Then, in a moment of clarity, we noted three things. First, in a visit to the Valley in January 2011, Dr. W. Stephen McBride, a Kentucky-based archaeologist and historian of the American Civil War, noted that Ringgold Barracks in Starr County "was the best preserved nineteenth century fort in the United States"; following that, he went on to say, "Too bad no one is doing anything about its preservation or interpretation."[2] Second, we recognized that we were just entering the second

---

1. Portions of the material appearing here were published previously under the title "Creating the Rio Grande Valley Civil War Trail," in *Extra Studies in Rio Grande Valley History*, ed. Milo Kearney et al., vol. 14 (Edinburg/Brownsville: University of Texas Rio Grande Valley, 2016), 457–78.
2. W. Stephen McBride, personal communication with Skowronek, January 4, 2012.

year of the sesquicentennial observations of the American Civil War. In consulting most general histories of the US Civil War and even general histories of Texas, no one would know the dramatic story of the many Civil War events that took place along the lower Rio Grande or the complex history of ethnic tension, international intrigue, and the clash of colorful characters that mark the Civil War era in this region. And third, we noted that Texas was the only past member of the Confederacy (Alabama, Mississippi, Louisiana, Florida, Georgia, South Carolina, North Carolina, and Virginia) to not have an existing trail devoted specifically to the American Civil War. Certainly, we thought, our focus should be the American Civil War, and the time to strike was now.

Over the next four months, with the aid of then graduate student Samantha Bernard, we compiled information on more than forty sites and personalities associated with the conflict. Our research included forts, battlefields, historic structures, encampments, cemeteries, and abandoned townsites from the Gulf of Mexico to Laredo. Our plan was to create a web-based "virtual" trail with occasional wayside exhibits. We charted out the sites and laid out our arguments on August 15 in a proposal for $75,000 to the National Endowment for the Humanities, titled "The American Civil War and the Rio Grande Valley." Six weeks later, the federal government was closed and sequestration was initiated. Our proposal, and no doubt many others, was not funded.

With that news, we felt the opportunity had passed. The proposal was shelved until the summer of 2013, when the Development Office at UTPA asked if we had any unfunded projects that might be of interest to the history-minded Summerlee Foundation of Dallas. The proposal was pared back to $20,000 for a web-based trail with a paper map and trail guide and submitted. In October we learned that we would receive $7,500, a tenth of the original proposed amount. Over the next three months, we met with representatives from the City of Roma, the Brownsville Community Improvement Corporation, and Rio Grande City, and from them secured additional funding. This additional funding allowed us to proceed and bring together a group of like-minded community and professional supporters from across the region and country to discuss the feasibility and support for the creation of a Civil War trail.

Creating the Rio Grande Valley Civil War Trail

On May 22, 2014, less than one year before the sesquicentennial observations of the last land battle of the American Civil War (Palmito Ranch/Hill, in

Cameron County), a meeting was convened on the UTPA campus in McAllen, Texas. There were nearly fifty individuals representing federal, state, and local entities such as the National Park Service, the US Fish and Wildlife Service, Texas Tropical Trails, the Texas Historical Commission, the Texas Department of Transportation, the Cameron County Historical Commission, the Starr County Historical Commission, the Hidalgo County Historical Commission, Port Isabel Marketing, the Port Isabel Museum, the Brownsville Civil War Sesquicentennial Committee, the Brownsville Historical Association, the Sons of Confederate Veterans, the Museum of South Texas History, the Starr County Historical Museum, and the Zapata County Museum of History. These organizations joined other interested community members, as well as faculty and staff from the Universities of Texas Brownsville and Pan American, to discuss their interest in this undertaking. We were joined by three "project scholars" in Civil War history: Dr. Jerry Thompson, Texas A&M International Regents Professor; Dr. W. Stephen McBride, Director of Archaeology, Camp Nelson Civil War Heritage Park, Kentucky; and Dr. James Leiker, Director of the Kansas Studies Institute. This was a grassroots approach to consensus building. For the trail to exist and succeed, there needed to be "buy-in." This project did not fall under the sole jurisdiction of the Community Historical Archaeology Project with School (CHAPS) Program at the University of Texas Rio Grande Valley. We were not experts in the American Civil War and especially not in the local history surrounding the Civil War. Thus we did not ask the attending organizations to contribute monetarily to the trail—what we did request was their support to identify sites and prepare brief synopses of their significance.

All agreed that it was a good idea to "create" the trail for educational and economic reasons. There also was a consensus that to understand the American Civil War in this region, there would need to be consideration given to the Mexican Civil War between Benito Juarez and the reactionaries who had supported Emperor Maximilian. Furthermore, given its location in an area in South Texas where Spanish is the first language in 85 percent of households, all saw the need to make the trail bilingual to serve the need of the local populace. That meant everything had to be translated. Finally, during the meeting, a date for a teacher workshop and official launch for the trail was chosen in February 2015, only seven months in the future.

Also attending the meeting was web designer Perla Pequeño from the

UTPA Information Technology offices. She asked the attendees about how information on the web page should be presented. Elisa Flores and Danny Cardenas from Marketing and Creative Services discussed the trail guide/map and how it might appear. Dr. Nick Taylor discussed the creation of podcasts and our need to identify English and Spanish voice talents with a modulation and timbre that would enhance the aural quality of the production. Representatives of the National Park Service based at Palo Alto Battlefield National Park donated their OnCell mobile website as a platform for distributing the projected podcasts via telephone and mobile computing devices. The work of these individuals and organizations, though not directly compensated, was immense—probably representing more than $20,000 in time and effort—and was ultimately the reason this project has been so successful.

After breaking into groups by county, the attendees selected lead advisors for Webb, Zapata, Starr, Hidalgo, and Cameron counties, through which the majority of the trail traversed, and then spent several hours identifying sites. When they left, they were charged with providing us with a one-page synopsis for each site, event, or personage, and its significance in the Civil War and other information on the location, or other resources such as maps and historic or contemporary photographs. These were to be submitted by July 1. Five weeks later, more than fifty sites were identified and described with 250-word site narratives. With the help of the project scholars, the CHAPS Program team edited and in some cases rewrote for clarity the narratives for the sites. These were returned to the county lead advisor for vetting. Once complete, they were prepared to be uploaded to the Rio Grande Valley Civil War Trail web page (www.utrgv.edu/civilwar-trail).

To do all of this, more funding was needed. The Summerlee Foundation of Dallas was again approached for additional support. Based on what had been accomplished and the plans for the podcasts, translations, and map/brochure, they generously provided the CHAPS Program with a grant of $15,000. With this in hand, during the fall of 2014, Vanessa Mares, in consultation with longtime screenwriter David Carren, rewrote the narratives as scripts for the podcasts. These scripts and the original narratives were translated by Dr. José Dávila-Montes, then professor of Spanish translation, interpreting, and court interpretation at the University of Texas–Brownsville. With these completed, Ms. Mares and Ivan Herrera, under Nick Taylor's direction, produced the podcasts with Jeff A. Koch and Octavio Saenz providing the voice talent in English and Spanish, respectively.

By the end of November, the English portion of the Rio Grande Valley Civil War Trail web page went live. In January and February of 2015, the Spanish narratives, English-language podcasts, and bilingual map were complete. On February 27, 2015, a little more than nine months after the initial meeting, a workshop for teachers was held on the UTPA McAllen campus. More than fifty educators attended, and they shared their thoughts about how the trail might be integrated into their curricula. The next day, the Rio Grande Valley Civil War Trail was "officially" launched with a ribbon cutting on the UTPA campus in Edinburg. More than 275 attended a series of presentations and a Civil War living history camp.

Building on the Foundation

In the years since that "ribbon cutting," CHAPS Program team members have made dozens of presentations on the Rio Grande Valley Civil War Trail

Rio Grande Valley Civil War Trail ribbon cutting ceremony at the community launch event on February 28, 2015.

to more than a thousand people in the region and across Texas. In addition to this volume, another book titled *The Civil War on the Rio Grande, 1846–1876* (2019) brings together the Rio Grande Valley Civil War Trail Project Scholars and other researchers to explore in greater detail the Civil War era in the region. Five additional teacher workshops were conducted with great success. These workshops have continued to focus on incorporating materials relating to the trail into K–12 classrooms. At the workshop held in February 2016, teachers interacted with the CHAPS Program team and other regional specialists to discuss the creation of traveling trunks filled with Civil War era artifact replicas for use in hands-on learning exercises. At the one held in February 2017, a complete set of forty lesson plans written to state-mandated student learning outcomes incorporating the trunk and the online trail, prepared by CHAPS Program team member Dr. Rolando Avila, was distributed to teachers. Following that workshop, the Summerfield G. Roberts Foundation of Dallas granted the program $17,665 in order to produce twenty trunks for distribution to local school districts. These activities have won significant recognition for the CHAPS Program and for the Rio Grande Valley Civil War Trail, including in 2016 the President's Achievement Award for Public Engagement from the Texas Historical Commission, and in January 2017 the Daniel G. Roberts Award for Excellence in Public Historical Archaeology from the Society for Historical Archaeology. Later in the spring of 2017, the 85th Texas State Legislature honored the CHAPS Program for outstanding public service for the Rio Grande Valley region by passing House Resolution 479.

Future Directions for the Rio Grande Valley Civil War Trail

In future years, the only limits to the Rio Grande Valley Civil War Trail will stem from a lack of imagination and vision. As the economy in South Texas shifts away from commercial agriculture to manufacturing and service industries, with an increasingly educated populace, cultural experience opportunities will become more and more viable. For decades the salubrious climate has attracted "Winter Texans" and others such that the region already boasts a vibrant ecotourism focus. Heritage tourism will put a spotlight on the unique history of the region. It is in conjunction with that vision that this volume has been produced. We have also looked to colleagues in "business" and "marketing" to use the trail as a focal point for "hands-on" education. Their students will work with local and regional chambers of commerce and economic development corporations across the five counties through which the trail passes. Students and scholars in history, anthropology, biology, and geology will continue to study the region and trail under the umbrella of the CHAPS Program.

For the trail to thrive, it must evolve. We envision "affiliated" restaurants and lodgings that will offer "discounts" to those who follow the trail. There will be adaptive reuse of historic structures. Sites in the City of Roma or the Ringgold Barracks in Rio Grande City may host a "bed and breakfast," "living history programs," "educational programs for students," "stables," "archaeological projects," "shops," and "restaurants." Buses, which once carried visitors to Nuevo Progresso or Reynosa, may now take Winter Texans and other visitors on heritage tourism excursions up and down the Valley. If the adage "If you build it, they will come" is to ring true in the Rio Grande Valley, we need scholarship to continue hand-in-hand with economic development. The Rio Grande Valley Civil War Trail is the first undertaking of its kind to link the two hundred miles from Laredo to Brownsville. May it serve as the launching pad for public history across the region.

Rio Grande Valley Civil War Trail Contributors Committee, May 2014.

Acknowledgments

The CHAPS Program at the University of Texas Rio Grande Valley (UTRGV) would like to thank all of the regional community partners who have played an integral role in this project. Their thoughts, input, and participation have helped to lay the foundation for the Rio Grande Valley Civil War Trail. Without their assistance, this book would not have come to fruition. On May 22, 2014, forty-three members of the Contributors Committee took the bold step to endorse the creation of the Rio Grande Valley Civil War Trail. They are (front row from left to right) Russell Skowronek, UTRGV CHAPS Director and Professor of History/Anthropology; Valerie Ramirez, Hidalgo County Historical Commission/Juneteenth Coordinator; Amparo Montes-Gutierrez, Curator of the Zapata County Museum of History; Virginia Gause, UTRGV Media and Marketing Librarian (retired); Karen Fort, Rio Grande Valley author and museum exhibit designer; Lendon Gilpin, Texas State University; Mark Allen, UTRGV graduate student; Roseann Bacha-Garza, UTRGV CHAPS Program Manager; Maria Elia Ramos, Starr County Historical Museum; Nancy Deviney, Texas Tropical Trails Executive Director; (second row from left to right) Stephen Walker, Texas Department of Transportation District Landscape Architect; Robert Ramirez, Nuevo Santander Press; Christopher Miller, UTRGV Professor of History and Codirector of the CHAPS Program; Manuel Hinojosa, Port Isabel Preservation Architect; Rolando Garza, National Park Service Resource Manager, Palo Alto Battlefield; George Gause, UTRGV Special Collections Librarian (retired); Tom Fort, Museum of South Texas History Senior Historian; Mark Spier, National Park Service Superintendent, Palo Alto Battlefield/Padre Island; James Leiker,

Johnson County Community College and Kansas Studies Institute Director; Elisa Flores, The Studio at UTRGV Account Services Manager; Samuel Ramos, Starr County Historical Museum; Wilson Bourgeois, Brownsville Civil War Sesquicentennial Chairman; Eran Garza, Peñitas Historical Society; (back row from left to right) Noel Benavides, Starr County historian; Jerry Thompson, Civil War historian/author and Texas A&M International Regents Professor; Bryan Winton, Santa Ana Wildlife Refuge Manager; James Mills, UTRGV Lecturer in History; Anthony Zavaleta, Professor of Anthropology, University of Texas Brownsville (retired); Jeff Cortinas Walker, Rio Grande Valley writer/columnist; Scot Edler, Lower Rio Grande Valley National Wildlife Refuge Assistant Manager; W. Steve McBride, Camp Nelson Civil War Heritage Park Director of Archaeology; Daniel Cardenas, The Studio at UTRGV Graphic Designer; Doug Murphy, National Park Service Chief of Interpretation, Palo Alto Battlefield; Norman Rozeff, Cameron County Historical Commission Secretary; Jack Ayoub, Texas Heritage and Independence Celebration Association; Craig Stone, Brownsville Historical Association/Sons of Confederate Veterans Commander Camp 2216.

Missing from photo are Hidegardo Flores, Zapata County Museum of History Director; William McWhorter, Texas Historical Commission, Coordinator of Military Sites Program; Alonzo Alvarez, Starr County Historical Commission President; Jeanie Flores, Port Isabel Museum Director; Elisa Beas, Rio Grande City Deputy City Manager; Toni Nagel, King Ranch Museum Director; and Frances Isbel, Hidalgo County Historical Commission.

Thanks to President Guy Bailey, past provost Havídan Rodriguez, interim provost Patricia McHatton, and Deputy Provost Cynthia Brown of the University Texas Rio Grande Valley for their support of our work. Also, thanks are due to Dean Walter Diaz and Assistant Dean Monica Denny of the College of Liberal Arts; Kimberly Selber, Elisa Flores and Daniel Cardenas of the Studio/Marketing Services; Velinda Reyes and Felipe Salinas of the Division of Institutional Advancement; Perla Pequeno and Russell Dove of Information Technology Services; and Sean Visintainer, who has begun to acquire historical documents that pertain to this project for UTRGV Special Collections and Archives. Thanks to Veronica Gonzalez and Richard Sanchez of the Division of Governmental and Community Relations for their part in the promotion of House Resolution 489, which honored the accomplishments of our program on the floor of the 85th Texas State Legislature.

Thanks also to Executive Director Shan Rankin, Curator of Collections and Registrar Dr. Lisa Kay Adam, and Archivist Phyllis Kinnison of the Museum of South Texas History. The museum houses primary source materials, photographs, and documents that have truly enhanced the research for this book. We'd also like to thank Captain Paul Matthews, Founder and Chairman of the Buffalo Soldiers Museum of Houston, and Naomi Carrier, Project Director and CEO of the Texas Center for African American Living History, for their support of our program and distribution of our materials. Special thanks are extended to Director Ethan Wright and Museum Specialist Chase Brazel of the Indiana War Memorial Museum in Indianapolis for providing access to and photographs of the 34th Indiana Volunteers' national and regimental colors.

We are eternally grateful to our sponsors for their continued support of the Rio Grande Valley Civil War Trail. We offer our gratitude to John Crain of the Summerlee Foundation of Dallas, David D. Jackson of the Summerfield G. Roberts Foundation of Dallas, Cori Pena of the Brownsville Community Improvement Corporation, Bobby Salinas of the City of Roma, and Elisa Beas of the Rio Grande City Economic Development Corporation for their financial contributions that have assisted in the development, enhancement, and sustainability of this project. Special thanks are due to Gene Krane and The Texas Historical Foundation for funds to cover expenses associated with the many illustrations that appear in this book.

We would like to thank John L. Nau III, chairman of the Texas Historical Commission, for touting our program's community engagement activities and the positive impact that our educational projects have had on the regional, state, and national communities. We extend further thanks to him for graciously supplying the foreword to this book.

We also recognize Dr. Rolando Avila as the author of most of the lesson plans that pertain to this project. Others were provided by Jose Perez of the South Texas Independent School District, and our colleague Dr. Megan Birk, Department of History, UTRGV. Mark Spier, Douglas Murphy, Rolando Garza, Karen Weaver, Daniel Ibarra, and Ruben Reyna of the National Park Service have contributed greatly to the reproduction of material items that pertain to the education of our regional K–12 students.

Many thanks go out to the descendants of Civil War era citizens who played some role in events that mark our Rio Grande Valley Civil War Trail. We thank Clara Dina Hinojosa and Judge Federico Hinojosa, Dr. Arnulfo Garza-

Vale, and Sam Vale for their assistance with our research and images that grace the pages of our publications and website.

Thanks to the many organizations throughout the Rio Grande Valley that have invited us to speak to their groups and promote awareness of the Rio Grande Valley Civil War Trail. They are the US Department of Veterans Affairs, the Texas Historical Commission's Texas Tropical Trails, Las Porciones Society of Edinburg, the Daughters of the American Revolution, the United Daughters of the Confederacy, the Sons of Confederate Veterans, the Nuevo Santander Genealogical Society, McAllen Public Library, McAllen Old Timers Club, and the Annual Juneteenth Observances–Restlawn Cemetery of Edinburg, Texas.

Many thanks to Elizabeth O. Skowronek of North Carolina State University for her help with some of the graphics in this book. Many thanks also to Dean Walter Diaz and the College of Liberal Arts for supporting this project. We also wish to acknowledge Rachel Paul for her excellent copy editing and indexing of this book.

Blue and Gray on the Border

Introduction

How to Use This Book

The Rio Grande Valley Civil War Trail traverses parts of five counties bordering the Rio Grande and Mexico. While its central focus is the war years 1861–65, it contextualizes that conflict within the thirty years bracketing the Mexican-American War (1846–48) and the end of Reconstruction (1876). Those seeking the nuances of this entire period should consult *The Civil War on the Rio Grande, 1846–1876* (2019).

Travelers will find a general overview of this era in chapter 1 of this volume, "The Contested History of the Rio Grande Valley: Framing the Civil War Era." The specific people and sites described in this introductory chapter are discussed throughout the various sections of later chapters, all relating to the various "stops" on the Rio Grande Valley Civil War Trail. (Please refer to the book's index for specific page locations for these "stops.") Note that the illustrations appearing in this chapter are historic views of places and personalities. The events that are chronicled are broadly spread across the two hundred mile length of the trail. Thus it behooves visitors to have a basic grasp of the history before venturing out to explore the region, as sites that are chronologically similar may be geographically distant.

Chapters 2 through 6 detail events and sites in Cameron, Hidalgo, Starr, Webb, and Zapata counties. Basic information on the history of each county is provided. These are illustrated with contemporary images. We recognize that readers will find certain redundancies in the text in these chapters. Most travelers will probably not explore the route in its totality, and because the route is not chronological, each site entry has to be able to stand alone. Information on the location of each site is provided, as well as the text of historical markers. Podcast information for sites on the Taylor and Rio Grande Valley Civil War Trails is also provided.

Chapter 7 focuses on the US Colored Troops (USCT) who served at the Battle of Palmito Ranch and later at sites the length of the trail, and more generally on the formation and role of the USCT in this era. Information is also provided on Camp Nelson, a Union recruitment and training center for the USCT in Kentucky, and the Buffalo Soldiers National Museum in Houston.

Chapter 8 looks beyond the northern bank of the Rio Grande to Civil War–related sites elsewhere in Texas. Mexican sites and personalities associated with this era are also found therein.

1

The Contested History of the Rio Grande Valley:
Framing the Civil War Era

The Spanish and Mexican Rio Grande Colony, 1749–1844

From a European point of view, for centuries the region we are calling the Lower Rio Grande Valley was an unsettled and unsettleable wasteland. From the time of Hernán Cortés's conquest of Mexico in the 1520s, the Spanish frontier along the Gulf of Mexico stopped at the site of the modern-day city of Tampico. What lay beyond was truly a no man's land called *Seno Mexicano* (Mexico Bay). Lack of interest in settling this region stemmed from a number of causes. First and foremost among these was the geophysical nature of the area itself. Largely a flat coastal plain, the region was extremely arid and largely inhospitable for human life, or at least for human life as Spaniards defined it. Native American groups roamed across the land in either nomadic or seminomadic fashion, harvesting wild plants and animals. In addition, many Indian groups from the colonized parts of Mexico took advantage of the lack of a Spanish presence in the area, fleeing into the region to escape Spanish enslavement.

Spanish indifference to the region came to an end, however, late in the seventeenth century. In 1685, while war raged between Spain and France, a French party under the command of René-Robert Cavelier, Sieur de La Salle, came ashore within the confines of Seno Mexicano. The failure of La Salle's

Figure 1.1. Sculpture of José de Escandón, University of Texas Rio Grande Valley, by Roberto Garcia Jr.

enterprise, along with the end of the war between Spain and France, brought an end to the immediate threat, allowing authorities in Mexico City to again neglect the territory. However, war with England, beginning in 1739, restored the fear that a foreign power might gain a foothold between Spain's active settlements in Northern Mexico and those between the San Antonio River and the Gulf of Mexico.

In response to this threat, a *Junta General de Guerra* (war council) was convened to consider plans for establishing Spanish control over the region. One of the principle players in the planning that followed, Juan Rodríguez de Albuerne, Marquis of Altamira, promoted sending a young but very well-established military commandant, José de Escandón, to stage a full-scale exploration of the, until then, unexplored Seno Mexicano. He ordered seven different armed detachments from seven separate colonial settlements in Mexico to move simultaneously toward the mouth of the Rio Grande, and in just over a month in early 1747 the grand exploring expedition had finished its work. Not only had the entirety of Seno Mexicano been mapped and settlement sites surveyed, but miraculously given the severity of the land and the hostility of its inhabitants—human, plant, and animal alike—not a single life had been lost.

In his final report to the Junta, Escandón proposed that the region be called *Nuevo Santander*, named after his home province in Spain.

Escandón envisioned an initial planting of fourteen settlements in Nuevo Santander. To populate these *villas* (villages), he advertised for settlers, giving priority to those from the seven posts that had provided men for the 1747 entrada. In addition to soldiers, he specified that he wanted colonists with frontier living experience and specific skills, including ranching and farming, as well as building crafts and even maritime skills. By the time the colonizing expedition came together late in 1748, nearly 700 families showed up to make the trek into the new territory; by the end of 1755, six villas that would form the core for settlement on the Rio Grande itself—Reinosa (later Reynosa), Revilla, Mier, Camargo, Dolores, and Laredo—had been established. Later, in 1774, ranchers who had settled downriver from Reynosa banded together to establish a villa near the mouth of the river, a community initially called San Juan de los Esteros Hermosos, later renamed Refugio.

Settlements on both sides of the river continued to grow, subsisting on small agricultural fields where irrigation was possible, but more commonly by trading beef tallow and cow, sheep, and goat hides for agricultural products imported from the Mexican interior. Although the region was virtually devoid of the sorts of mineral wealth that Spaniards generally prized—gold and silver in particular—it did possess one mineral in abundance: salt. The presence of salt in large quantities facilitated the tanning industry and also made possible profitable dried meat and fish exporting, as well as exporting the salt itself, especially to the mining areas in the Sierra Madre Oriental to the southwest.

Although the attainment of independence by Mexico from Spain in 1821 changed a great deal in the nation generally, life in the Lower Rio Grande Valley changed very little. The Mexican government reconstituted the province of Nuevo Santander into the free state of Tamaulipas, but more importantly, the villa of Refugio would henceforth be known as Matamoros and was designated as an official port for international trade. By 1830 the town had grown to nearly seven thousand residents—Mexican, European, and North American—and its monthly tax revenues exceeded one hundred thousand pesos by 1832, making Matamoros the largest town on Mexico's northern frontier.

While mercantile activities became increasingly important on the southern stretch of the Rio Grande, traditional ranching continued to dominate life farther upstream. Enormous ranches surrounded the old villas of Laredo, Revilla,

Figure 1.2. Matamoros, circa 1843. Color lithograph published in John Phillips's *Mexico Illustrated in Twenty-Six Drawings by John Phillips and A. Rider, with Descriptive Letterpress in English and Spanish* (London: publisher not identified, 1848, plate 26). Photo courtesy of Dorothy Sloan-Rare Books Inc., Austin, Texas.

and Dolores. In 1830, Jesús Treviño, a former resident at Revilla, began a new settlement, San Ygnacio, building a fortified sandstone home that served as a ranch house and provided shelter during Indian raids and other disturbances of the peace. At Laredo, descendants of the villa's founder, Tomás Sánchez de la Barrera y Garza, especially the Benavides family, continued to exercise significant control, both politically and economically. Between 1827 and 1848, Basilio Benavides virtually ruled the town and surrounding countryside.

While things were mostly prospering along the river, the northern portion of the old Seno Mexicano continued to live up to the region's reputation before Escandón's settlements. The territory between the Rio Grande and Nueces River was particularly prohibitive to settlement. Early travelers making their way overland to the now booming city of Matamoros gave ample testimony to the still unsettled region that the Spanish called *El Desierto Muerto* (the dead desert). The single exception to its abandoned character was the remarkable number of wild horses that resided along the coastal plain, leading Americans (especially those who risked both natural and bureaucratic threats by entering Mexican territory to round up these broncos) to call the region the Wild Horse Desert.

Following Mexican independence, the area to the north of El Desierto Muerto, the province of Coahuila y Tejas, became a popular destination for settlers from the United States. In an effort to put a barrier between hostile Comanche and Apache Indians and the productive settlements along the Rio Grande and farther inland, the Mexican government allowed so-called empresarios such as Stephen F. Austin to bring in migrants, many of whom were from the American South. In a story far too familiar to bear retelling here, these foreign settlers grew increasingly restive under Mexican rule, often ignoring Mexican laws and customs altogether. Finally, in 1835, a mostly Anglo-American group began a revolution against Mexican authority, fighting a war for independence that lasted until April 1836, when, in the Battle of San Jacinto, Mexican President Antonio Lopez de Santa Anna was captured by Texas troops. In order to gain his freedom, Santa Anna signed the Treaty of Velasco, which hinted that the boundary between the newly established Republic of Texas and Mexico would be the Rio Grande. However, the Mexican government refused to ratify the treaty, leaving the question of the boundary unresolved. Mexico considered the former southern boundary of Coahuila y Tejas, the Nueces River, to be the actual border, while many in Texas asserted control all the way to the Rio Grande.

One point of contention between Texans and the Mexican government that helped lead to the independence movement had been Santa Anna's 1835 suspension of the Federalist Constitution of 1824. This was the cause of much dissention throughout Northern Mexico, but especially in the highly independently minded former Nuevo Santander. Texas' eventual success in attaining independence left Tamaulipans without support in their struggles against the centralizing tendencies of Mexican Conservatives. This led to the establishment of the Republic of the Rio Grande. A number of longtime Rio Grande political actors, including Jesús de Cárdenas, Antonio Canales Rosillo, Antonio Zapata, José María Jesús Carbajal, and possibly Laredo mayor Basilio Benavides, the uncle of later Confederate commander Santos Benavides, led the movement. They held a convention in January 1840, at which they declared independence from Mexico and claimed for its territory the areas of Tamaulipas and Coahuila, north to the Nueces and Medina rivers, setting their capital at Benavides's town of Laredo. The republic survived only until November, when it was crushed by the Mexican Army. Many of the leaders who survived, however, came away from the experience even more rigidly opposed to centralized authority and loyal to the idea of states' rights—a factor that undoubtedly shaped reactions when the issue would arise again.

The Mexican War and a New Social Order, 1845–1860

The boundary between Texas and Mexico became a matter of great significance when annexation negotiations between the Republic of Texas and the United States of America began. In 1838, Sam Houston, the hero of the Battle of San Jacinto and by then president of the Republic of Texas, invited the United States to annex Texas. While many Americans were eager to acquire such a huge expanse of new territory, smoldering political contentions over slavery came into play. Former US president John Quincy Adams, now a Whig member of the House of Representatives, filibustered for three weeks against the acquisition of such a massive block of potential slave territory. Seeking to avoid national controversy, Congress refused to ratify the annexation treaty, and the question of Texas statehood was postponed. In 1842 Houston repeated his invitation to the United States, but yet again politics prevented any resolution. Finally, however, in 1843, President John Tyler appointed fellow Virginian Abel P. Upshur as secretary of state, who immediately reopened the matter of Texas annexation. Negotiations between Houston's representatives and Upshur (at first, and then, after Upshur's death, John C. Calhoun) led to a treaty of annexation on April 11, 1844. But annexation remained a major arguing point between proslavery and antislavery forces, and the treaty failed ratification in the Senate. The matter refused to die, however, and Texas loomed large during the presidential campaign later that year. Democratic candidate James K. Polk vowed to defend the territorial claims of Texas, and his resounding victory led Congress to pass a joint resolution to annex Texas in the following February. Significantly, the annexation agreement recognized the Treaty of Velasco and the Rio Grande boundary for the new US-Mexico border.

Many Mexicans pointed out that the Treaty of Velasco had been signed under duress, and Mexico's popular press demanded renegotiation. The Mexican government agreed, threatening war. Late in 1845, President Polk dispatched John Slidell to Mexico City to negotiate the boundary dispute while simultaneously dispatching American troops to Louisiana, ready to strike if Mexico resisted Slidell's offers. Nervous but bristling over what seemed to be preparations for war, the Mexican government refused to receive Slidell, leading Polk to order troops from New Orleans toward the Rio Grande. Arriving there in

April 1846, Gen. Zachary Taylor built an earthen fort on the northern shore of the river overlooking Matamoros. He called the installation Fort Texas and left it under the command of Maj. Jacob Brown. For their part, the Mexican government reached an end to its patience; on April 22 Mexico proclaimed that its territory had been violated and declared war. Then, on May 8, at a site near Matamoros called Palo Alto, that contestation would escalate into all-out war when the troops under Taylor's command were attacked by Mexican forces as they ferried supplies to Fort Texas. The battle lasted for two days and was then followed by a second one at Resaca de la Palma. Meanwhile, Mexican troops in Matamoros also began shelling the fort, leading to the death of Major Brown. Shortly thereafter, the US Congress declared war, and a general invasion of Mexico was planned.

Just over seventeen months later, Mexico City fell to an American army, and the war came to an end with an all-out victory for the United States. In the treaty that finally ended the conflict, the 1848 Treaty of Guadalupe Hidalgo, the United States finally set the southern boundary of Texas at the Rio Grande. Seeking to solidify the legitimacy of the border and also to secure the region from disorder, the government launched the construction of a string of forts along the river. Fort Texas, now called Fort Brown after its fallen commander, stood at the mouth of the river. About a hundred miles upriver, troops began the construction of post at Davis Landing that would eventually be called Fort Ringgold, after another Mexican War hero, Bvt. Maj. Samuel Ringgold. Two years later, another post was established near the old colonial villa of Laredo, Fort McIntosh, named for Lt. Col. James S. McIntosh, another casualty of the war. Then, about another hundred miles upriver, the army established Fort

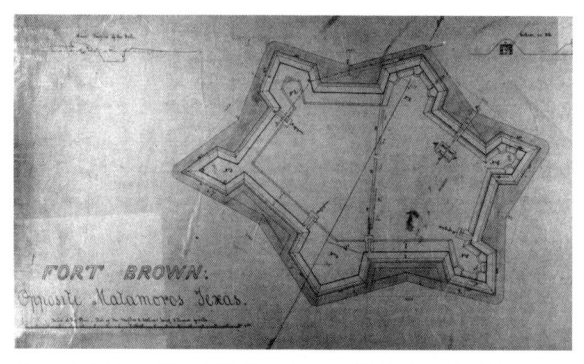

Figure 1.3. Plan of the 1846 Fort Brown. US National Archives.

Duncan, named for war casualty James Duncan. These were all situated at long-standing popular river crossing points, and squads of troops frequently patrolled the areas between them, seeking to pacify the region.

In the new and more stable environment along the Lower Rio Grande, adventurous Anglo- and Irish-American capitalists like Richard King and Mifflin Kenedy, veterans of the Mexican-American War, joined the community. These newcomers joined merchant-adventurers such as Charles Stillman, who had settled in Matamoros when the port first started booming in the 1830s. Immigrants also became established merchants, traders, and ranch owners, like Swede John Vale, Irishman John McAllen, and Scotsman John Young. In the 1850s, mixed race families such as the Webbers, Jacksons, Brewsters, Rutledges, and Singleterrys also settled in the region. Escaping from the cruelties of racism and slavery in the American South, these families sought refuge in this still highly contested region and established enclaves where, within a ferry ride to freedom, they could enjoy some sense of security.

While some of the old original Spanish families welcomed these newcomers—some even married the daughters of leading Mexican landowners and business leaders—not all was peaceful. Before the Rio Grande had been recognized

Figure 1.4. John McAllen/Salomé Ballí McAllen, circa. 1865. Courtesy of McAllen Ranch Archives.

as the legal boundary, local landowners' holdings often spanned the river, creating extraordinarily complicated title issues. In addition, the substitution of US common law standards for the traditional Mexican legal codes made many residents nervous about their continued economic status. In February 1850, there was even talk in Brownsville that the Americans would annul all the land titles throughout the region. In a number of instances, the original owners were forced into expensive litigation and ruinous lawsuits to defend their property.

One glaring example of such outrages was the case of María Estéfana Goseascochea de Cortina, who was forced to sacrifice thousands of acres of land to her attorneys to defend her claims. One of the beneficiaries of her travails was the aforementioned Charles Stillman, who purchased a large tract from one of Goseascochea de Cortina's sons and set about to build the Texas city of Brownsville, which had come into existence around Fort Brown. Another of Goseascochea de Cortina's sons, Juan Nepomuceno Cortina, claimed that this was an act of fraud. This simmering of discontent exploded into the Cortina War in the summer and fall of 1859. Twice Cortina and his guerilla army,

Figure 1.5. Juan Nepomuceno Cortina in 1865. Cortina is a descendant of the original Spanish land grantee, Blas María de la Garza Falcón, who settled the ranch that later became the City of Rio Grande City, Texas. Courtesy of Jerry D. Thompson.

Figure 1.6. John Salmon "Rip" Ford in frontier apparel. Daguerreotype in frame. Courtesy of the John N. McWilliams Texas Ranger Collection.

numbering as many as six hundred, defeated the Brownsville militia and the Texas Rangers, one of the few times the Rangers were ever defeated in battle. It was not until December 1859 that a combined force of Rangers and US Army regulars decisively defeated Cortina at Rio Grande City and drove him into Mexico.

In one final blow against his enemies, Cortina attempted to capture the steamboat *Ranchero*, owned and operated by two of his antagonists, Richard King and Mifflin Kenedy, only to be defeated again on February 4, 1860, in the Battle of La Bolsa. As a result of Cortina's activities, then Col. Robert E. Lee visited the Ringgold Barracks in 1860, conducting investigations at the commandant's quarters, which would later be known as the Robert E. Lee House. Cortina then remained in Mexico, only to return when the Civil War opened new opportunities to pursue old grievances.

Following the skirmish at La Bolsa, Brownsville and Matamoros finally quieted after the six months of chronic violence. The threats and mayhem had paralyzed the two sister communities. Brownsville's population, which stood at 4,000 people in 1852, had dwindled to 2,734. The majority of the inhabitants were families composed of naturalized citizens or Mexicans, but a large coterie remained European, especially French, Spanish, Italian, German, and English. These families spoke more than one language, and up to four languages could be heard on the street on a regular basis; regional newspapers were published in English and French, English and Spanish, and sometimes in all three languages. While ranchers in outlying areas remained cautious, hiring private managers and security to maintain their herds and properties, the merchants in the towns welcomed the brief modicum of peace.

The Civil War, 1861–1865

Just as it appeared that things were settling down along the Rio Grande, political developments in faraway regions of the United States threatened to upset the communities again. In the presidential election of 1860, upstart Republican candidate Abraham Lincoln faced three opponents: mainstream Democrat Steven Douglas, Southern Democrat John C. Breckinridge, and the moderate Constitutional Unionist John Bell. Lincoln's three challengers split a large portion of the electorate among themselves, leaving Lincoln with a vast advantage in the Electoral College. More to the point, however, was the fact that his electoral majorities came exclusively from Northern and Western states, where antislavery sentiments were strong. Southerners recoiled in horror, fearing that the victorious Republicans would immediately end slavery and ruin the Southern economy and society. Throughout the South, meetings were held to determine the proper response, and finally, during December 1860 and January 1861, six states declared their intention to secede from the Union: South Carolina, Mississippi, Florida, Alabama, Georgia, and Louisiana. On February 4, 1861, delegates from the six seceding states, and from Arkansas and Tennessee, met in Montgomery, Alabama, and formed the Confederate States of America.

At first, Texas demurred from joining the rebellion. Elder statesman and governor Sam Houston was a staunch unionist and used all the persuasion at his disposal to convince his younger colleagues to be patient. Ignoring Houston, a number of Confederate sympathizers, including the chief justice of the Texas Supreme Court, John Salmon "Rip" Ford, moved ahead to call a secession convention, which met on January 28, 1861. On the following day, the convention voted overwhelmingly to join the Confederacy; however, at Houston's insistence, they decided to submit the resolution to a popular referendum. That decision brought the issue squarely into the local politics of the Lower Rio Grande Valley.

Most of the political leadership in the region favored secession—surprisingly inasmuch as the area had virtually no slaves, though undoubtedly many still remembered the states' rights arguments from the Republic of Rio Grande debacle. But in Zapata County there was a strong contingent of voters who wanted to keep Texas in the Union. On the eve of the referendum voting, local judge Isidro Vela made it known that anyone who failed to vote in favor of secession would be fined fifty cents, a considerable sum for poor farmers eking out a living in the small villages along the river. The ploy seemed to work: officials announced that the vote for secession was unanimous, 212 to 0. However, when Vela learned that several individuals had not voted and others publicly protested the legitimacy of the vote, Vela ordered them arrested. The result was a full-fledged revolt.

On April 12, 1861, the day before the surrender of Fort Sumter in the harbor of Charleston, South Carolina, forty armed Tejanos and Mexicanos under the leadership of a thirty-nine-year-old ranchero named Antonio Ochoa seized control of the southern part of the county and proclaimed a pro-Unionist stance. Some of Ochoa's followers had ridden with Juan Cortina during the Cortina Wars and were tired of the abuse and discrimination that Cortina had fought against. Eventually the men were confronted by Judge Vela, who persuaded them to return to their homes. Meanwhile, Henry Redmond, a key vassal in the Benavides political machine in Zapata County, was in a state of panic. Holed up at his fortified ranch near San Bartolo, Redmond sought reassurance from now colonel John S. "Rip" Ford, who was commanding Confederate forces at Fort Brown. Ford assured Redmond that the troops at Laredo under Capt. Santos Benavides were more than capable of protecting him and the other Zapata County officials. In his turn, Benavides dispatched troops downriver from Fort McIntosh. Emboldened, Judge Vela quickly issued arrest warrants for Ochoa and eighty of his men. With little hesitation, the Confederate troops marched for Rancho Clareño, where Ochoa was said to have his headquarters, reaching the small river village before daylight on April 15. Outnumbered and caught off guard, Ochoa's men tried to surrender, but they never had a chance. Many were gunned down where they stood, while others were killed as they fled toward the river. With that, the Civil War began in the Rio Grande Valley.

In the days following the massacre at Rancho Clareño, unsubstantiated rumors rapidly spread along the Rio Grande that Cortina had formed an alliance with Union authorities and was reported to be marching on Carrizo to avenge the victims of the Clareño massacre. Heeding the rumors, Colonel Ford sent Santos Benavides personally downriver to assist the Zapata County officials. By

Figure 1.7. Colonel Santos Benavides Ramon, highest-ranking Hispanic in the Confederate Army. Courtesy of the Ursuline Sisters Collection, Webb County Heritage Foundation Archives.

the morning of May 21, 1861, Cortina and seventy of his men had Benavides completely surrounded at Redmond's Ranch. On the following morning, a company of reinforcements from Laredo ran into a party of Cortina's men near San Bartolo, and a skirmish ensued. Hearing the sounds of gunfire, Benavides and his men galloped out of Redmond's Ranch to join the fray. Cortina also heard the sounds of battle and pushed his men forward. In a running fight that lasted forty minutes, Benavides and thirty-six of his men completely routed Cortina's raiders. Having vowed to take no prisoners, Benavides ordered eleven men, some of whom were badly wounded, to be shot where they lay. The wily Cortina, however, successfully escaped across the river.

The conflicts in Zapata County set the tone for most of the rest of the war. Many who sympathized with Ochoa flocked across the river to join up with Cortina. Others fled the area for Louisiana, where they formed Union companies in exile. Those who favored the Confederate cause also formed independent companies who coordinated their activities with Benavides in Laredo and Ford in Brownsville. Most folks, however, including the mixed-race families who had come into the region in the 1850s, tried to stay out of the fray. Various skirmishes took place during 1862, including an attack on a Confederate supply wagon train at Roma and a Confederate attack at Soledad, but for the most part armed conflicts were relatively rare.

This does not mean, however, that the war had only minimal impact on the region. While battalions of uniformed men were facing off in Virginia and elsewhere in the east, another Civil War was shaping up in the Rio Grande Valley. Taking advantage of the chaos in the United States, Conservatives in Mexico sought to replace the Liberal government led by Benito Juárez with a more elitist regime under their control. They sought assistance from allies in Europe, and in December 1861, Spanish troops invaded the Mexican port of Vera Cruz. A couple of weeks later, British and French warships arrived to reinforce the Spanish. Though it appears that at least the British and Spanish were concerned primarily with collecting outstanding debts owed to them by Mexico, the French monarch Napoleon III had much more ambitious goals: he sought nothing less than the reestablishment of a French presence on the North American mainland and the creation of a political and cultural counterweight to the dominant British and Anglo-Americans. Given assurances that the Mexican people would favor it, the French began marching westward from Veracruz. On April 19, 1862, the Brit-

Figure 1.8. Benito Juarez/Emperor Maximilian. Library of Congress.

ish and Spanish ships at Veracruz set sail for home, thus separating themselves from the would-be conquerors. Although Mexican forces under the command of Gen. Ignacio Zaragoza repelled the invasion at the famous May 5, 1862, Battle of Puebla, now celebrated as Cinco de Mayo, the French returned in 1863 with a far larger force, and on May 17 took Puebla and soon thereafter entered Mexico City. On April 10, 1864, Ferdinand Maximilian Joseph von Habsburg received the crown offered by a carefully selected assembly of Mexican Conservatives, beginning the Mexican Imperium. Liberals, now calling themselves *Juáristas*, were forced to flee and began a civil war of their own.

Now two civil wars raged along the Rio Grande, both of which would be shaped by one of the key points in the 1848 Treaty of Guadalupe Hidalgo. In addition to fixing the Rio Grande as the international boundary, the treaty also established the river as an international waterway. What this meant in terms of international law was that neither Mexico nor the United States could interfere with traffic on the river or with ships departing from the river into the Gulf of Mexico for up to eighteen nautical miles offshore. Under normal circumstances, this did not present much of a problem, though it made smuggling between the two countries difficult to control. But now with Texas in a state of war with the United States and another civil war raging in Mexico, noninterference with shipping became a potentially serious problem.

At the outset of the war, Lincoln's chief military strategist, Winfield Scott, had outlined what was ridiculed in Northern newspapers as the "Anaconda Plan." Designed to bring the Confederacy to its knees economically, Scott's plan called for the systematic naval blockade of the entire Southern coast to be accompanied by penetration of the Mississippi Valley from both the north and south. With its maritime traffic paralyzed, it was Scott's belief that the Confederacy would soon have to surrender. But as an international port, Matamoros, in officially neutral Mexico, was off-limits from Union blockading.

As the war progressed, the Union blockade became increasingly effective, and with the fall of New Orleans early in 1862, Southern cotton growers became desperate to find outlets for their crops. They found it on the Lower Rio Grande. Aboard Union vessels on blockade duty just beyond the eighteen nautical mile limit, captains and crews watched in frustration as foreign ships arrived, discharged cargo and loaded bales, and then weighed anchor and departed. In international waters, Union warships could and did stop and search foreign-flag vessels suspected of trading with the Confederates through

Figure 1.9. The War in Texas—Brownsville, now occupied by the army under Maj. Gen. Nathaniel P. Banks, showing Santa Cruz Ferry. From a sketch by L. Avery, 1863. Retrieved from the Library of Congress, https://www.loc.gov/item/97519142/.

Mexico. The majority had their manifests and documents in order, maintaining that their inbound cargoes were consigned to Mexican merchants, and their outbound cotton was Mexican in origin. Unless a US Navy skipper was prepared to question the authenticity of the documents and perhaps spark an international incident, there was little more he could do except permit the merchant vessel to sail on. Further complicating matters, to the official Imperial government in Mexico, the running of Confederate cotton out of Matamoros and the arrival of arms, ammunition, and other military supplies for the Southern cause was completely acceptable, as it would keep the United States from intervening in Mexican affairs. On the other hand, they wanted to be sure that similar military supplies were kept out of the hands of the Juáristas. Meanwhile, Union commanders were entirely favorable to letting arms get to the rebels in Mexico, but dead set against them getting into the hands of Texas Confederates. In the resulting chaos, economic opportunists rose to the occasion, taking advantage of all sides in the scramble for wartime profits.

Throughout 1862, Matamoros and the neighboring fishing village of Bagdad became the outlet for international cargoes and the port of entry for war materiel that would feed both civil wars. Here and in Brownsville operated the renowned photographer Louis de Planque, whose photographs of Confederate, Union, and Imperialist leaders and soldiers provide a glimpse into this remote yet cosmopolitan corner of the American Civil War (see fig. 4.4). Also during the war, Corpus Christi journalist Henry A. Maltby established a newspaper called the *American Flag* in Brownsville, specifically to promote the Confederate cause to foreign audiences. Increasingly, cotton began arriving on carts and wagons from as far away as Louisiana and Arkansas and was exchanged for arms, ammunition, salt, and other strategic resources that would be hauled back across the coastal plain or into the Mexican interior. Longtime local business figures such as Richard King, Mifflin Kenedy, John Vale, and Charles Stillman established warehouses and counting houses in Matamoros, Brownsville, neighboring Clarkesville, and Bagdad and upriver in Rio Grande City and Roma to cash in on the trade. And with Texas in Confederate hands and Mexico in the hands of Maximilian, there was virtually nothing the Union could do about it.

By the autumn of 1863, the Union had had enough; Lincoln and Chief of Staff Henry Halleck ordered Gen. Nathaniel P. Banks, then in command of the Union Department of the Gulf, to make an amphibious landing along the Texas coastline near Brownsville, with an eye toward capturing the city and closing down the trade. On November 2, Banks landed a force of seven thousand men at Brazos Island and established a secure foothold. Col. William Dye's 2nd Brigade soon began marching toward Brownsville. The city itself, under the military command of Brig. Gen. Hamilton Prioleau Bee, was being defended by a mere four companies from the 33rd Texas Cavalry under Col. James Duff and

Figure 1.10. Brig. Gen. H. P. Bee, C. S. A. DeGolyer Library, Southern Methodist University, Lawrence T. Jones III Texas Photographs.

Figure 1.11. *Cotton Trails* sketch by Tom A. Fort. Courtesy of Margaret H. McAllen Memorial Archives, Museum of South Texas History.

another two companies of local three-month volunteers. A Confederate cavalry company under Capt. Richard Taylor sent to observe Dye's movements was dispersed by the numerically superior Union force, which then marched unopposed into Brownsville at around 10:00 a.m. on November 6, 1863. General Bee ordered the immediate evacuation of the city and abandoned Fort Brown. He personally supervised the burning of what military supplies and cotton he could. Inside the fort was eight thousand pounds of explosives that detonated, causing a terrifying explosion. Between the explosion and the burning of strategic materials, fire began spreading throughout the city, causing enormous disorder. General Banks finally arrived on the scene in the late afternoon to take official command.

This military loss had a profound impact on the cotton trade and other commercial activities throughout the entire region. With the coastal wagon route closed by Union forces, any cotton traffic was forced to shift inland to upriver sites such as Rio Grande City and Roma. Banks sought to counter this shift by dispatching a wing of his force upriver, where they took possession of Fort Ringgold in Rio Grande City. Banks also ordered a contingent under his command to the Confederate salt works at La Sal del Rey, which were destroyed.

With Rio Grande City and Roma in Union hands, increasingly the cotton traffic shifted to the inland towns of Laredo and Eagle Pass, which remained in Confederate hands. Hoping to put an end to this activity as well, a Union force of two hundred men marched upriver with the intention of seizing Laredo and capturing the large inventories of cotton rumored to be there. On March 19, 1864, a Confederate scout under the command of Col. Santos Benavides spotted the advancing federals outside of Laredo. Benavides rallied his small Confederate force of merely seventy-two men, barricaded several of the streets with cotton bales, and placed snipers on the buildings around St. Augustine Plaza. At 3:00 p.m. the federals dismounted on the bank of Zacate Creek at the edge of the city and advanced. A furious firefight erupted that lasted for more than three hours, with Union troops advancing three times and being driven back by Benavides's small force each time. Unable to seize the village in the growing darkness, the Union soldiers rapidly withdrew some two miles downriver and went into camp for the evening. Union casualties are uncertain, but it is known that none of Benavides's defenders were killed or wounded. Laredo remained in Confederate hands.

Following this failed attempt, Union strength in the Lower Rio Grande Valley began to decline. As the war heated up on other fronts, men increasingly were diverted from Fort Brown and other posts along the river. This opened up an opportunity for a Confederate counteroffensive, and in June 1864, Col. John S. "Rip" Ford and Cristobal Benavides led a force downriver from Laredo. Learning that the Confederate force was nearing Brownsville, Capt. Phillip Temple rode with one hundred troops of the Union 1st Texas Cavalry to the Las Rucias Ranch, about twenty-four miles west, hoping to take Ford's sixty-man force by surprise. But Ford had added troops from the 4th Arizona Cavalry and arrived at Las Rucias with 250 men. In a short battle, the Confederates

Figure 1.12. USCT Digging trenches on the north end of Brazos Island. *Frank Leslie's Illustrated Newspaper*, 1864.

pinned down the Union troops in the ranch headquarters, and then routed the federals, killing twenty, wounding twenty-five, and taking thirty-six prisoners. Exhausted and short on supplies, Ford stopped his march to regroup. By the time he had amassed sufficient resources to resume, Union commander Francis J. Herron had ordered Brownsville abandoned. Troops withdrew to Brazos Island, where they dug in for the remainder of the war. Brownsville and the Rio Grande were again in Confederate hands.

Over the course of the following year, things along the Rio Grande resumed their previous pattern, with foreign ships and cargoes arriving regularly and Confederate cotton moving out into world markets. Union troops at Brazos Island occasionally skirmished with the Confederates patrolling out of Fort Brown, but there were no major battles. The Union presence continued to hamper traffic on the coastal wagon road, but shipments continued to upriver ports, and steamers ferried cargoes back and forth on the Rio Grande.

On April 9, 1865, Gen. Robert E. Lee surrendered his Army of Northern Virginia to Gen. Ulysses S. Grant at Appomattox Court House, Virginia. This marked the end of significant fighting in the most costly war in US history, but many Confederate commanders west of the Mississippi had not yet accepted the Union's victory. It was also rumored that many Confederate politicians and military leaders might head for Texas to either stage a last stand or possibly flee into Mexico to establish a government in exile. Whether for these or other reasons—the matter is still hotly debated—on May 11, Col. Theodore H. Bar-

Figure 1.13. Battle at Palmito Ranch as depicted by artist Clara Lily Ely. Courtesy of Texas Southmost College Library.

rett, commander at Brazos Island, ordered Lt. Col. David Branson to lead 250 men of the 62nd US Colored Infantry and 50 men of the 2nd Texas Cavalry toward the remaining Confederate strongholds along the river. Branson's force advanced to Palmito Ranch, and on May 13, bolstered by Barrett himself and 200 men of the 34th Indiana Infantry, pressed steadily onward toward Brownsville. The arrival of John S. "Rip" Ford with 300 Confederate cavalrymen and several artillery pieces halted Barrett's advance near the western edge of Palmito Ranch. The Union infantry fell back to the coast, and as darkness fell, an artillery bombardment by Union naval ships held the Confederates at bay and allowed the federals to escape. Casualties in the battle were relatively light, with the Confederates counting ten men wounded and the Union six wounded and two killed. One of the dead was Pvt. John Jefferson Williams of the 34th Indiana Infantry, who earned the sad distinction of becoming the final battlefield fatality in America's bloodiest war.

Reconstruction and Beyond, 1866–1906

Months before the battle at Palmito Ranch, Lincoln had dispatched Gen. Lewis "Lew" Wallace to the Rio Grande to investigate the military status of the region. Though not officially charged with the power to negotiate any sort of truce, Wallace met with and forged an informal armistice with

Brownsville commandant Gen. James E. Slaughter, which makes Barrett's motives for marching out of Brazos Island all the more questionable. In any case, following the battle, things in the Lower Rio Grande Valley settled into a lull, pending an official end to the conflict. Edmund Kirby Smith, commander of the Confederate Trans-Mississippi District, was hesitant to surrender, but finally on June 2, 1865, he yielded to Union general Edward R. S. Canby. The Civil War in Texas was now over. On June 19 ("Juneteenth"), Gen. Gordon Granger arrived in Galveston and issued General Order No. 3, which officially ended slavery in Texas.

However, the war's end did not ensure a reign of peace in the Rio Grande Valley. As had been anticipated when Richmond fell to Grant's forces in April, many Confederate military and political leaders were making their way into Mexico. Encouraged by Mexican Emperor Maximilian, colonies such as the one at Carlota, between Mexico City and Vera Cruz, drew men such as former Texas Governor Pendleton Murrah, who took up residence in Monterrey, not far from the Rio Grande border, where another large colony grew up. Whether or not these colonies intended to continue the war, the danger was certainly real. In addition, civil war continued to rage in Mexico and frequently spilled over the river into South Texas. Beyond that, the military and political unsettledness in the region had encouraged Apache and Comanche groups to raid settlements in quests for horses, slaves, and honor. It was clear to many that the region would have to be put under military authority immediately.

On May 30, 1865, a large Union military force marched into and occupied Brownsville. Among them was a detachment of the 62nd Colored Infantry, itself part of the much larger United States Colored Troops (USCT). Formed by General Order No. 143 on May 22, 1863, over the remainder of the war, the USCT came to number roughly 179,000 enlisted men and noncommissioned officers—African Americans were not allowed full military commissions and were led by white officers. Three regiments of the USCT had entered the Rio Grande Valley in the fall of 1864 and formed the backbone of the Union force encamped at Brazos Santiago. Over the course of May 1865, nearly sixteen thousand USCT veterans of the XXV Corps arrived at Brazos Island from City Point, Virginia, and were quickly dispersed to Fort Brown at Brownsville, Ringgold Barracks at Rio Grande City, Fort McIntosh at Laredo, and Fort Duncan at Eagle Pass, as well as to smaller posts scattered along the border. These men would form the literal army of occupation in the Rio Grande Valley.

The posts along the Rio Grande were far from being up to the job of housing a large, continuing military force. As noted, Fort Brown had been largely destroyed by fire and a powder explosion when it was seized by Union forces in 1863. Forts Ringgold and McIntosh were little more than frontier outposts manned by local vaquero volunteers. It fell to the USCT to begin constructing permanent buildings. At Fort Brown, they immediately began erecting brick buildings, including a new commandant's quarters, elegant officers' quarters, and a base hospital. Similar construction was begun soon afterward at Ringgold and McIntosh. In between these anchor forts, African American troops also built smaller bivouac sites at places such as White's Ranch in Cameron County, upriver from Fort Brown; Edinburg in Hidalgo County; Roma in Starr County; and various ranches in Zapata County. Patrols frequently moved between these many sites, watchful for cattle rustlers moving back and forth across the river, as well as Indian raiding parties and men seeking to smuggle both goods and weapons across the border.

Often such smuggled goods were bound for one side or the other in the continuing civil war in Mexico. On that side of the river, Imperialist forces were rapidly losing ground to Juárez's Republicans. On April 11, 1866, Napoleon III ordered all French troops in the interior to retreat to Mexico City and later advised Maximilian to give up the throne and return to Europe. Then, on June

Figure 1.14. Fort Brown Post Hospital, built in 1869—Gorgas Hall of Texas Southmost College.

2, Juárista general Mariano Escobedo inflicted a crippling defeat on the remaining Imperial forces in northeastern Mexico. At the battle of Santa Gertrudis/Cervalo, his combined force of 1,500 infantry and 500 dragoons destroyed the substantial forces escorting two supply convoys vital to a continued Imperial presence in Nuevo Leon and Tamaulipas. His troops killed 396 enemies, wounded 165, took hundreds of prisoners, and seized eight pieces of artillery and more than a thousand muskets while suffering 155 fatal casualties. The Rio Grande periphery of the empire soon crumbled, with the last Imperial troops departing Matamoros on June 23, 1866, and sailing from Bagdad two days later. This created an enormous power vacuum that various *caudillos* (strong men) sought to fill. In Matamoros, for example, in August 1866, Juárez ordered the arrest of Gen. Servando Canales for having abandoned the city in the face of an Imperial assault and sent Gen. Santiago Tapia to replace him. In response, Juan Cortina, who again was inserting himself into Rio Grande Valley affairs, declared himself governor of Tamaulipas. The two rebels joined forces. Following Tapia's death due to cholera, Juárez sent Escobedo to Matamoros in early November with orders to reestablish federal authority. Given the uncertain situation, the US consul in Matamoros requested a US force to protect American citizens and property. In response, Gen. Thomas Sedgwick sent nine companies of troops, consisting largely of USCT, into the city, where they remained until December 1, 1866.

Meanwhile, the Juáristas continued their attacks throughout Mexico. By early 1867, their ranks grew to some sixty thousand men, with their Imperialist foes now reduced to half that number. In April, twenty-eight thousand Juárista troops under the command of Gen. Porfirio Diaz liberated Mexico City after a lengthy siege. Maximilian then gathered his remaining forces in Querétaro, where he and seven thousand soldiers soon fell under siege. On May 15, Juárez announced the fall of Querétaro, and scarcely more than one month later, on June 19, 1867, the former emperor, Gen. Tomás Mejia, and Gen. Miguel Miramón fell before a firing squad.

The successful termination of the civil war in Mexico meant that many of the threats previously posed to peace along the border were at an end. As a result, the military presence in the Rio Grande Valley began to experience a serious decline. Through late 1866, more than half the regiments of the XXV USCT Corps mustered out. The last USCT regiment to depart the Valley, the 117th USCI, mustered out from Forts McIntosh and Ringgold in July 1867. This did not end the military presence along the border, nor the continued role of African American Troops. Forts Brown, Ringgold, and McIntosh continued to operate throughout the century, though with diminished numbers. As for the men of the USCT, during the summer of 1866, the US government reorganized the now peacetime army, authorizing two regiments of black cavalry, the 9th and 10th United States Cavalry, and six regiments of black infantry. In 1869 the black infantry regiments were consolidated into two units: the 24th and 25th United States Infantry. As with the USCT, these regiments were composed of black enlisted men, commanded, with a very few exceptions, by white officers. These would become the famed "Buffalo Soldiers" who patrolled the Great Plains, including Texas, throughout the Indian Wars of the late nineteenth century. Often divided into small company and troop-sized detachments stationed at isolated posts, the Buffalo Soldiers performed routine garrison chores, patrolled the frontier, built roads, escorted mail parties, and handled a variety of difficult civil and military tasks. They also participated in most of the major frontier campaigns of the period, including those in Texas against the Kiowas, Comanches, and Apaches. Often they were posted at Forts Ringgold and McIntosh as they pursued their missions.

In terms of the civil order in the region, it was restored more or less to what

Figure 1.15. Buffalo Soldiers by Frederic Remington, "Marching in the Desert with the Buffalo Soldiers," in "Scout with the Buffalo Soldiers," in *The Century: A Popular Quarterly*, 1889.

had been the status quo since the Spanish period. The haciendas created during the late 1700s remained a dominant economic institution. Despite having supported the Confederacy, men such as Richard King and Mifflin Kenedy invested large fortunes made during the war in land, where they followed the traditions of *patronismo* (patronialism) familiar to Spaniards and Mexicans. For his part, Charles Stillman took his money and ran, settling in New York City, where he founded the City Bank of New York (Citibank). Col. John S. "Rip" Ford, though left penniless at the end of the war, with the help of his Civil War contacts, won a position as the editor of the Brownsville *Sentinel* in 1869, later serving as the city's mayor. The two Tejanos who may have been most responsible for the outbreak and peculiar shape of the war in the Rio Grande Valley, Juan Nepomuceno Cortina and Santos Benavides, both lived until nearly the end of the century (1894 and 1891, respectively). Cortina continued to insert himself into affairs in the region until 1875, when President Porfirio Diaz summoned him to Mexico City, where he was to receive a pension and "permanent surveillance" in lieu of execution for his many past misdeeds. Benavides served three times in the Texas legislature from 1879 to 1884 and twice as an alderman of Laredo, built up his ranch and other business holdings, and in recognition for his loyalty to Juárez during the Mexican civil war, was made a special envoy to the United States in 1880.

Further Reading

Bacha-Garza, Roseann. "Race and Ethnicity along the Antebellum Rio Grande: Emancipated Slaves and Mixed Race Colonies." Chapter 4 in *The Civil War on the Rio Grande, 1846–1876* edited by Roseann Bacha-Garza, Christopher L. Miller, and Russell K. Skowronek. College Station: Texas A&M University Press, 2019.

Chance, Joseph E. *Jose María De Jesús Carvajal: The Life and Times of a Mexican Revolutionary*. San Antonio, TX: Trinity University Press, 2006.

Fort, Karen G., and Tom A. Fort. "Los Algodones—The Cotton Times on the Rio Grande." Chapter 7 in *The Civil War on the Rio Grande, 1846–1876*, edited by Roseann Bacha-Garza, Christopher L. Miller, and Russell K. Skowronek. College Station: Texas A&M University Press, 2019.

Garza, Rolando. "Archeological Insights into the Last Battle of the Civil

War: Palmito Ranch, May 12–13, 1865." Chapter 9 in *The Civil War on the Rio Grande, 1846–1876*, edited by Roseann Bacha-Garza, Christopher L. Miller, and Russell K. Skowronek. College Station: Texas A&M University Press, 2019.

Greaser, Galen D., Virginia H. Taylor, and William N. Todd. *New Guide to Spanish and Mexican Land Grants in South Texas*. Austin: Texas General Land Office, Archives and Records Division, 2009.

Jones, Oakah L. *Los Paisanos: Spanish Settlers on the Northern Frontier of New Spain*. Norman: University of Oklahoma Press, 1996.

Leiker, James N. "The Black Military Experience in the Rio Grande Valley." Chapter 10 in *The Civil War on the Rio Grande, 1846–1876*, edited by Roseann Bacha-Garza, Christopher L. Miller, and Russell K. Skowronek. College Station: Texas A&M University Press, 2019.

———. *Racial Borders: Black Soldiers along the Rio Grande*. College Station: Texas A&M University Press, 2002.

Levinson, Irving W. "Separate Wars and Shared Destiny: México and the United States from 1861 to 1878." Chapter 5 in *The Civil War on the Rio Grande, 1846–1876*, edited by Roseann Bacha-Garza, Christopher L. Miller, and Russell K. Skowronek. College Station: Texas A&M University Press, 2019.

Miller, Christopher L., "Prelude: From the *Seno Mexicano* Frontier to the Nueces Strip Borderland." Chapter 1 in *The Civil War on the Rio Grande, 1846–1876*, edited by Roseann Bacha-Garza, Christopher L. Miller, and Russell K. Skowronek. College Station: Texas A&M University Press, 2019.

McAllen, M. M. "Life Lived along the Lower Rio Grande during the Civil War." Chapter 3 in *The Civil War on the Rio Grande, 1846–1876*, edited by Roseann Bacha-Garza, Christopher L. Miller, and Russell K. Skowronek,. College Station: Texas A&M University Press, 2019.

———. *Maximilian and Carlota: Europe's Last Empire in Mexico*. San Antonio: Trinity University Press, 2015.

McBride, W. Stephen. "From the Bluegrass to the Rio Grande: Kentucky's United States Colored Troops on the Border, 1865–1867." Chapter 8 in *The Civil War on the Rio Grande, 1846–1876*, edited by Roseann Bacha-Garza, Christopher L. Miller, and Russell K. Skowronek. College Station: Texas A&M University Press, 2019.

Murphy, Douglas A. "To Occupy and Possess Our Own: The Mexican War, the Civil War, and the Fight for the Rio Grande Valley." Chapter 2 in *The Civil War on the Rio Grande, 1846–1876*, edited by Roseann Bacha-Garza, Christopher L. Miller, and Russell K. Skowronek. College Station: Texas A&M University Press, 2019.

———. *Two Armies on the Rio Grande: The First Campaign of the US-Mexican War*. College Station: Texas A&M University Press, 2014.

Thompson, Jerry D. *Cortina: Defending the Mexican Name in Texas*. College Station: Texas A&M University Press, 2007.

———. "Col. José de los Santos Benavides and Gen. Juan Nepomuceno Cortina: Two Astounding Civil War Tejanos." Chapter 6 in *The Civil War on the Rio Grande, 1846–1876*, edited by Roseann Bacha-Garza, Christopher L. Miller, and Russell K. Skowronek. College Station: Texas A&M University Press, 2019.

———. *Mexican Texans in the Union Army*. El Paso: Texas Western Press, 1986.

———. *Tejano Tiger: José de Los Santos Benavides and the Texas-Mexico Borderlands, 1823–1891*. Fort Worth: Texas Christian University Press, 2017.

———. ed. *Tejanos in Gray: Civil War Letters of Captains Joseph Rafael De La Garza and Manuel Yturri*. College Station: Texas A&M University Press, 2011.

———. *Vaqueros in Blue & Gray*. Austin: Presidial Press, 1976.

Thompson, Jerry D., and Lawrence T. Jones III. *Civil War & Revolution on the Rio Grande Frontier: A Narrative and Photographic History*. Austin: Texas State Historical Association, 2004.

Valerio-Jiménez, Omar S. *River of Hope: Forging Identity and Nation in the Rio Grande Borderlands*. Durham: Duke University Press, 2013.

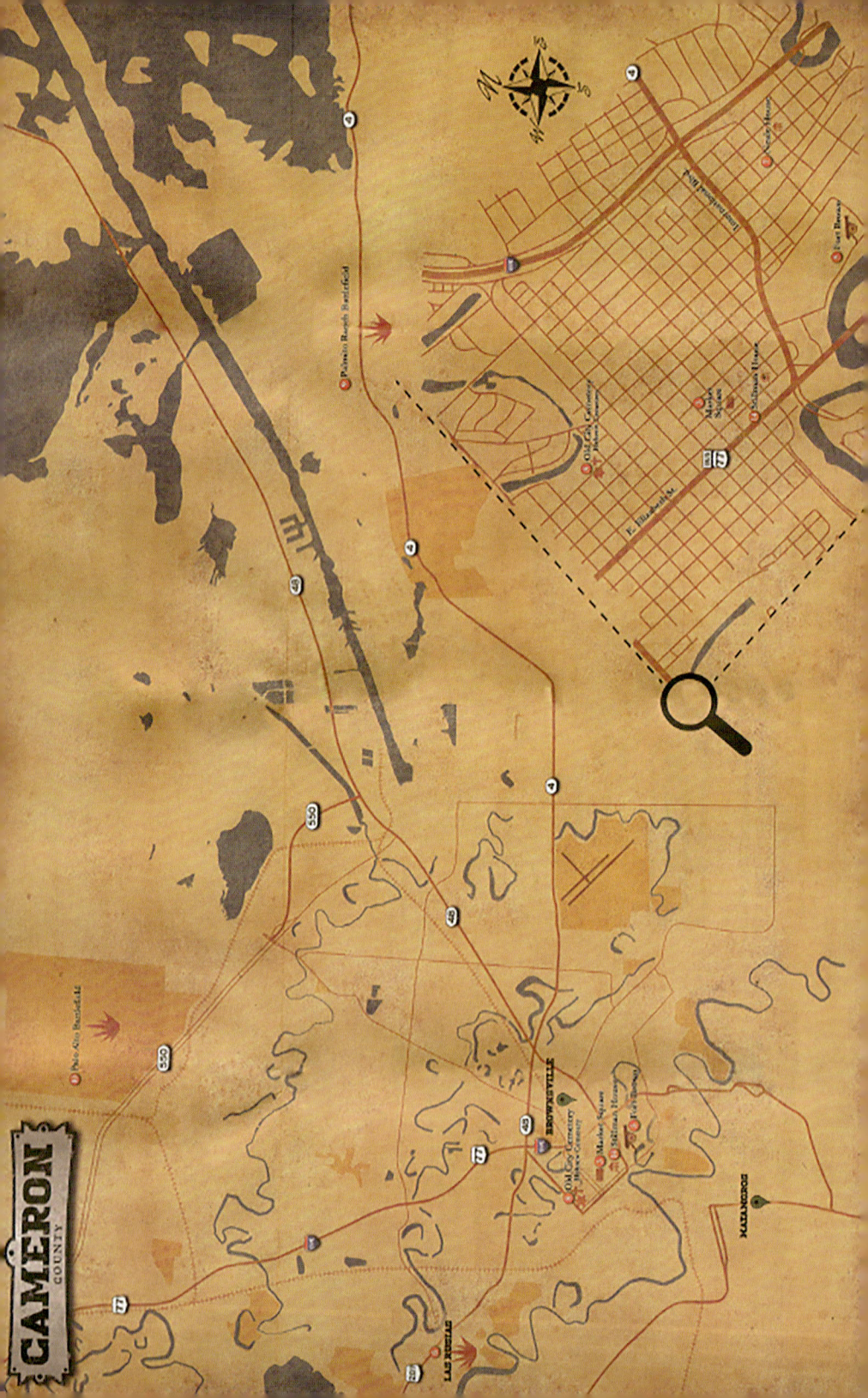

CAMERON COUNTY

2

Cameron County Sites and Events

Established in 1848 following the Mexican-American War, the county was named for Ewen Cameron, a soldier in the Republic of Texas who was executed in March of 1843 by the Mexican Army following an abortive attack on Mier, Tamaulipas. Bordering the Gulf of Mexico on the east, Willacy County on the north, Hidalgo County to the west, and Mexico to the south, Cameron County played a central role in the history of South Texas during the Civil War. To understand its significance, visitors should begin their exploration with the events associated with the Mexican-American War.

Visitors traveling the Rio Grande Valley Civil War Trail will find many sites to visit dating from 1846 to 1876. While some have been destroyed or are otherwise inaccessible, their stories are covered in local museums. As a result, we suggest four museums in the county to provide context for the events that transpired in Cameron County and the larger region: the Port Isabel Historical Museum at 317 East Railroad Avenue in Port Isabel, and in Brownsville, the Palo Alto Battlefield National Historic Park on 7200 Paredes Line Road, the Brownsville Heritage Museum located in the Stillman House at 1325 East Washington Street, and the Old City Cemetery Center at 1004 East 6th Street. In addition to the Rio Grande Valley Civil War Trail, visitors should follow the National Park Service's "Taylor's Trail Mobile Tour" (956–847–3002) to learn about the Mexican-American War. Also, those visiting Brownsville wishing to bike or hike portions of the historic district should follow the "Brownsville Historic Battlefield Tour" (956–241–2785, ext. 333) and the "Mitte Cultural District Heritage Trail" (956-541-5660). For ease of use, this chapter is divided into two sections: sites associated primarily with the Mexican-American War and sites associated with the American Civil War and later.

Mexican-American War

In July 1845, US president James K. Polk sent an army led by Gen. Zachary Taylor to Corpus Christi, on the banks of the Nueces River in what was then the Republic of Texas. Five months later on December 29, 1845, a joint resolution of the US Congress was passed and signed by President Polk, annexing Texas as a state in the Union. Six weeks later on February 14, 1846, the Republic of Texas relinquished its sovereignty to the United States. Mexico disputed the legality of the United States annexation of their breakaway province, noting that Texas' historic southern boundary was the Nueces. Texas and the United States did not agree, and in January 1846, President Polk ordered General Taylor to claim the Rio Grande as the US boundary. In March, Taylor led four thousand troops across dozens of Mexican land grant ranches to the river's edge, and there, across from Matamoros, began construction of the earthen redoubt known as Fort Texas. In response, the government of Mexico sent an army under the command of Gen. Mariano Arista to Matamoros. This move would lead to the Mexican-American War.

Figure 2.1. General Zachary Taylor's headquarters, Santa Maria, Texas, 1845. Courtesy of Robert Engstler (Purple Heart recipient) and Oralia Rodriguez.

Palo Alto Battlefield National Historic Park

In Cameron County there are five sites associated with the Mexican-American War: Port Isabel, Fort Texas, Rancho de Carricitos, Palo Alto, and Resaca de la Palma. This important aspect of United States and Mexican history is interpreted by the National Park Service at Palo Alto Battlefield National Historic Park. Visitors are urged to begin their exploration at the park, where bilingual exhibits and an excellent film explain the run-up to the Mexican-American War and its ramifications for both the United States and Mexico. Then follow the all-weather trail to the battlefield to see where the events of May 8–9, 1846, unfolded. Be certain to take advantage of the Taylor's Trail Mobile Web (956–847–3002) during your visit to this and related sites. Furthermore, this and many of the sites relating to the Mexican-American War in Brownsville are connected by the Brownsville Historic Battlefield Trail, which allows visitors to hike and bike through history.

TEXAS HISTORICAL COMMISSION—MARKER #5289
BATTLE OF PALO ALTO
Was fought here May 8, 1846 and was won by the Army of the United States.

Figure 2.2. Cannon at Palo Alto Battlefield National Historic Park.

Cameron County Sites and Events

Location: The park is located at the northeast corner of the intersection of FM 1847 (Paredes Line Road) and FM 511/FM 550, approximately 5 miles north of Brownsville, Texas.

GPS Coordinates: Latitude 26 01' 00.66" N Longitude 97 28' 45.56" W
Access: A unit of the National Park Service. The visitor center is open daily from 8:00 a.m. to 5:00 p.m. and is closed Thanksgiving Day, December 25, and January 1. Visitors will find handicapped accessible restrooms, a bookstore, and paved trails. There is neither food nor water available for purchase.

Admission Fee: None

Contact: 956-541-2785, ext. 333

Taylor's Trail Mobile Web: 956-847-3002; Extensions: 100, 101, 102, 103, 104, 105, 106, 107, 108, and 109

Fort Texas/Brown

Constructed in April of 1846 by the US Army, the remaining earthen fortifications are the only standing structures dating from the Mexican-American War

Figure 2.3. Map to show regional battles during the Mexican American War era. Courtesy of the National Park Service.

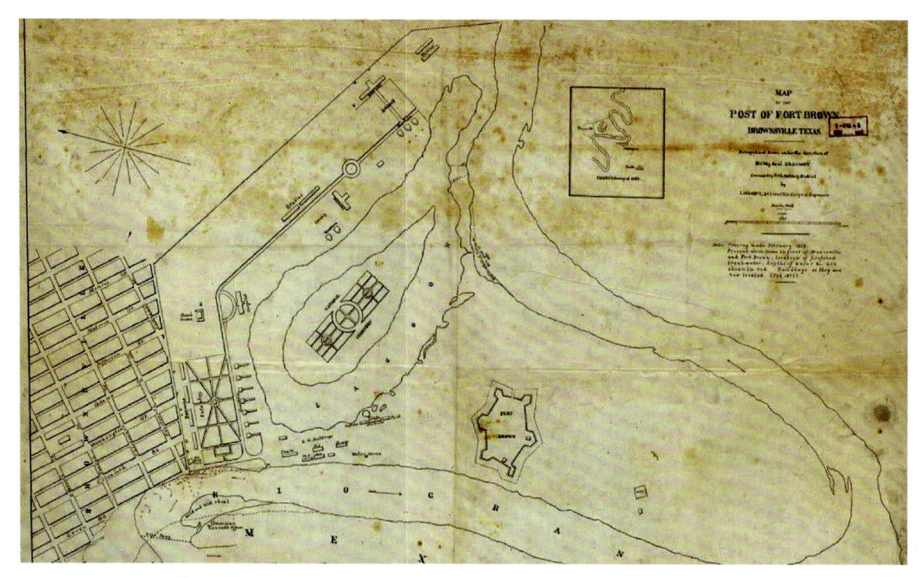

Figure 2.4. Detail of the six-sided star-shaped earthworks footprint layout of Fort Brown. Map of the Post of Fort Brown, Brownsville, Texas, 1877. US National Archives.

Figure 2.5. Upright cannon at Fort Brown earthworks.

37

in the United States. Built in the shape of a six-sided star, each earthen face of the fort was from 125 to 150 yards long. The walls were 9 feet high and 15 feet wide and were encircled by a moat 20 feet wide and 8 feet deep. Inside, a number of bomb-proof chambers and powder magazines were constructed to provide shelter from enemy bombardment. On May 3, the Mexican Army began shelling the fort from across the Rio Grande. The siege lasted five days. During the attack, Maj. Jacob Brown, the fort's commander, was mortally wounded. The fortification was subsequently named in his honor.

The remains of the original earthen fortifications are located on land belonging to the International Boundary and Water Commission. Visitors to the site will see a large muzzle-loading gun planted muzzle up in the midst of the surviving earthworks. The gun's trunnions are marked with the casting date, 1837, and the letters "WP F" for the West Point Foundry.

TEXAS HISTORICAL COMMISSION—MARKER #1971
FORT BROWN, TEXAS

Fort Taylor, renamed Fort Brown, May 17, 1846, in honor of Major Jacob Brown, 7th Infantry, who died here May 9, 1846, in its defense. Garrisoned by the 7th Infantry with Companies "I" 2nd Artillery and "E" 3rd Artillery. Original dimensions: Earth work of 800 yards perimeter, 6 bastion walls 9½ feet high, parapet 15 feet wide, ditch 8½ feet deep, 15 to 20 feet wide

Location: 300 River Levee Road, Brownsville, TX 78523. Located just south of Texas Southernmost College and the University of Texas Rio Grande Valley Brownsville campus on Riverside Levee Drive off of University Boulevard.
GPS Coordinates: Latitude 25° 53' 46.86" N Longitude 97° 29' 18.59" W
Access: There are no facilities on-site.
Taylor's Trail Mobile Web: 956-847-3002; **Extensions:** 300, 301, 302, and 303

Rancho de Carricitos (Thornton Skirmish)

On the morning of April 25, 1846, Capt. Seth Thornton's party of 63 US Dragoons, based at Fort Texas (later Fort Brown), approached this ranch. They were investigating reports that a large Mexican force had crossed the river the previous day. The dragoons spotted a small cluster of houses within the clearing and decided to investigate. There they encountered Mexican gen-

Figure 2.6. Historical marker complex at Rancho de Carricitos at the site of the Thornton Skirmish, 1846.

eral Anastasio Torrejón, with 1,600 cavalry and infantry troops. In the ensuing clash, eleven US soldiers died, and forty-six, including Captain Thornton, were taken prisoner. This incident started the Mexican-American War.

TEXAS HISTORICAL COMMISSION—MARKER #5478
THORNTON SKIRMISH
The spot where "American blood was shed on American soil," April 25, 1846; here Captain Seth B. Thornton and 62 dragoons were attacked by Mexican troops.

Location: At 15376 Highway 281 "Military Highway" (San Benito) on the north side of the thoroughfare west of Los Indios and near Las Rusias, Texas, between Weaver and Cannon Roads, approximately 25 miles west of Brownsville, Texas.
Access: There are no facilities on-site.
Taylor's Trail Mobile Web: 956–847–3002; **Extensions:** 400, 401, 402, 403, and 404

Resaca de la Palma
Following the retreat from Palo Alto on May 9, 1846, Gen. Mariano Arista and his army occupied this site in force. Gen. Zachary Taylor and his troops followed Arista's force from Palo Alto to the old resaca. Arriving at Resaca de la

Figure 2.7. Entrance marker and cannon at Resaca de la Palma battlefield site, Brownsville.

Palma around 3:00 p.m., the US troops immediately attacked. In less than an hour, the battle was over with the Mexican Army defeated. Administered by the National Park Service as a unit of Palo Alto Battlefield National Historic Park, the site features a walking trail, interpretive waysides, and a picnic area. Gates are open Tuesday through Saturday, 9:00 a.m. to 3:00 p.m.

> **TEXAS HISTORICAL COMMISSION—MARKER #328**
> **BATTLE OF RESACA DE LA PALMA**
> Was fought here May 9, 1846, and the defeat of the Mexican Army under General Mariano Arista by the United States troops under General Zachary Taylor made good the claim of Texas to the territory between the Nueces and the Rio Grande.

Access: There are no facilities on-site.
Taylor's Trail Mobile Web: 956-847-3002; **Extensions:** 200, 201, 202, 203, 204, and 205

American Civil War and Reconstruction
Palo Alto and the American Civil War
The prairie of Palo Alto and the nearby field of Resaca de la Palma were scenes of a battle from the Mexican-American War, but the sites also have significance

to the Civil War. Dozens of young officers who experienced some of their first combat in the clashes with Mexican troops on May 8–9, 1846, moved up to positions of leadership in the Civil War. Ulysses S. Grant, George Gordon Meade, Don Carlos Buell, and twenty-one others became generals in the Union Army (table 1). James Longstreet, John Pemberton, and twelve more of their peers became generals in the Confederate ranks (table 2). Edmund Kirby Smith, who was a lieutenant at Palo Alto, later commanded the Trans-Mississippi Department of the Confederacy, which included Texas and the Rio Grande Valley.

Table 1. American commissioned officers who served at Palo Alto and Fort Brown in May of 1846, who later served as general officers in the Union Army during the Civil War

Name	Killed in Action
Benjamin Alvord	
Christopher Columbus Augur	
Joseph K. Barnes	
William Thomas Harbaugh Brooks	
Robert Christie Buchanan	
Don Carlos Buell	
Napoleon Jackson Tecumseh Dana	
Lawrence Pike Graham	
Ulysses Simpson Grant	
John Porter Hatch	
Alexander Hays	Wilderness, VA, May 5–7, 1864
William Hays	
Henry Moses Judah	
George Archibald McCall	
Joseph King Fenno Mansfield	
Randolph Barnes Marcy	
George Gordon Meade	
William Reading Montgomery	
Gabriel Rene Paul	
John James Peck	

Cameron County Sites and Events   41

Name	Killed in Action
Thomas Gamble Pitcher	
Alfred Pleasanton	
Joseph Haydn Potter	
John Fulton Reynolds	
Israel Bush Richardson	Antietam, MD, September 17, 1862
John Cleveland Robinson	
Charles Ferguson Smith	
George Henry Thomas	
Seth Williams	
Thomas John Wood	

Francis E. Heitman, *Historical Register and Dictionary of the United States Army from Its Organization, September 29, 1789 to March 27, 1903* (Urbana, IL: 1965).

Table 2. American commissioned officers who served at Palo Alto and Fort Brown in May of 1846, who later served as general officers in the Confederate Army during the Civil War

Name	Killed in Action
Barnard Elliott Bee	Bull Run/Manassas, VA, July 21, 1861
Braxton Bragg	
Arnold Elzey	
Franklin Gardner	
Robert Selden Garnett	Corricks Ford, WV, July 13, 1861
Richard Caswell Gatlin	
William Joseph Hardee	
Theophilus Hunter Holmes	
Bushrod Rust Johnson	
Edmund Kirby Smith	
Lewis Henry Little	
James Longstreet	

Name	Killed in Action
John Porter McCown	
Lafayette McLaws	
John Bankhead MacGruder	
John Clifford Pemberton	
Gabriel James Rains	
Daniel Ruggles	
William Steele	
Carter Littlepage Stevenson	
David Emanuel Twiggs	
Lloyd Tilghman	
Earl Van Dorn	

Francis E. Heitman, *Historical Register and Dictionary of the United States Army from Its Organization, September 29, 1789 to March 27, 1903* (Urbana, IL: 1965).

Although the battlefields did not witness fighting during the Civil War, the Palo Alto prairie was a camp site for Union forces in the autumn of 1863 when they arrived to seize control of the Rio Grande. The 37th Illinois Volunteer Infantry, bivouacked there on their way to the occupation of nearby Brownsville. The sites also had great symbolic value for these Union soldiers who (though a generation later) well remembered battles during the war with Mexico. Maj. Augustus Pettibone of the 20th Wisconsin Volunteers captured the thoughts of many of his peers when he wrote home to explain the invasion of the Rio Grande delta: "We have come," he said, "as armed citizens of the Union to occupy and possess our own, to recover the soil for which our elder brothers fought and bled in the war with Mexico, and to once more unfurl the ensign of the republic along this southwest border, made historic ground for all time by the battles of Palo Alto and Resaca de la Palma."[1]

Rio Grande Valley Civil War Trail Mobile Web: 956-847-3002; **Extension:** 2012

---

1. H. Pettibone Maj. XX Wisconsin Volunteers to "Friend Lockwood," 12 November 1863, printed in *Cleveland Morning Leader*, 16 December 1863.

Brazos Island

Once a small low barrier island in southernmost Texas that played an important role in the Civil War, Brazos Island does not appear on modern maps. Although the Rio Grande in the nineteenth century could support steam boat traffic, a sandbar at the mouth of the river prevented large oceangoing ships from entering its deeper inland waters. The solution was to unload these vessels at Brazos Island and ferry their cargoes upriver. During the Mexican War, Gen. Zachary Taylor established a military depot on the island's north end. Following Texas' secession from the Union, Confederate troops seized the port. Union naval ships tried to halt the trade through Brazos Island as part of its blockade of the Confederate coast, a strategy that forced the Confederates to shift their commerce to Bagdad, across the river in the Mexican state of Tamaulipas. Nonetheless, until Union forces occupied the island in November 1863, it remained a haven for blockade runners. At that time, Union general Napoleon Dana landed his troops at the depot and fortified it before pursuing his conquest of the Rio Grande Valley. Confederate troops eventually pushed back, but a small US force held Brazos Santiago for the remainder of the war. After Confederate leaders in Texas surrendered in May 1865, Union forces, primarily US Colored Troops, used Brazos as their landing and staging point for postings in the interior. A major storm in 1867 destroyed most of the depot's structures. The Brazos depot was never rebuilt, and its remains eventu-

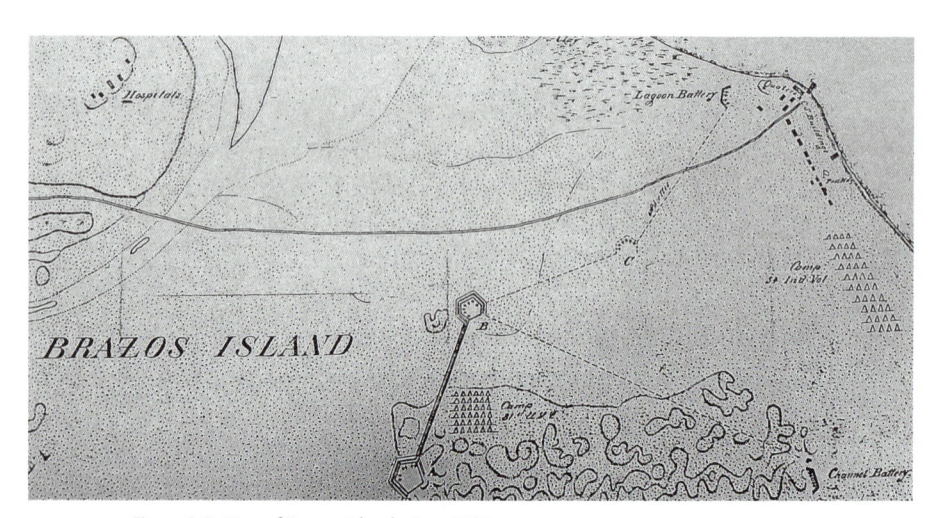

Figure 2.8. Map of Brazos Island, circa 1866.

ally disappeared under coastal dunes. Following Hurricane Beulah in 1967, portions of the depot were uncovered. Artifacts recovered from the site of the depot are now on display at many local museums.

TEXAS HISTORICAL COMMISSION—CIVIL WAR CENTENNIAL MARKER #496 BRAZOS SANTIAGO, C.S.A.

Brazos Santiago Pass, to south of this spot, was important Confederate harbor-entry during the Civil War. On island across the pass were fort and town of Brazos Santiago, where on Feb. 21, 1861, Texas troops under Col. John S. Ford captured the U.S. depot with mortars, siege guns and ordnance. A Confederate battery was then set up. In March 1861, off the bar, on U.S.S. "Daniel Webster," E. B. Nichols and Maj. Fitzjohn Porter, acting for Texas and the U.S., arranged Federal evacuation of the Rio Grande. Blockade ships arrived Dec. 1861. Col. Ford shifted forces to Brownsville. Gen. J. B. Magruder, C.S.A., ordered blasting of lighthouse north of pass, 1862. Trade vital to Confederacy plied from Cuba, Europe, Asia to Bagdad, Mexico, often actually slipping into Brazos Santiago Pass. Harbor sheltered blockade runners 1861–64. On May 10, 1863, U.S.S. Brooklyn destroyed schooners in the harbor. Late 1863, French warships banned war material in Bagdad, and Mexican steam lighters ran guns from sea vessels into Brazos Santiago. Nov. 2, 1863, Gen. N.P. Banks landed U.S. Army here, took line of Rio Grande forts. Refortified Brazos Island and made it terminus for Army railroad to Rancho Blanco on Rio Grande. When C.S.A. retook Rio Grande Line in 1864, Federals in Brownsville were thrown back to Brazos Island. Col. Theodore H. Barrett, with troops from here, marching on Brownsville in May 1865, was confronted by Col. Ford's Confederates at Palmito Hill and fought last engagement of the Civil War.

Location: Brazos Island was formerly a barrier island south of Padre Island, at the south end of the Laguna Madre. Now a narrow peninsula connected to the mainland, Brazos Island State Scenic Park (measuring 1 square mile) is located on this site.
GPS Coordinates: Latitude 26° 01′ 53.92″ N Longitude 97° 09′ 37.58″ W
Access: The park is always open and contains 1,000 acres. Although owned by the State of Texas, there are no facilities available for visitors.
Rio Grande Valley Civil War Trail Mobile Web: 956-847-3002; **Extension:** 2002

TEXAS HISTORICAL COMMISSION—MARKER #11777
BRAZOS SANTIAGO PASS AND BRAZOS ISLAND MILITARY DEPOT

Named by the Spanish, Brazos Santiago Pass is a narrow passageway extending inward from the sea. The pass lies between Brazos Island and Padre Island. The changing depths of the pass channel kept large vessels from entering, but offered seclusion to smaller ships. The entire area proved strategically important in a variety of military conflicts. Brazos Santiago harbor became part of the Texas revolution when the Texas warship "Invincible" heavily damaged the Mexican warship "Bravo" in April 1836. Supplies bound for the Mexican Army did not reach their destination. In 1846, U.S. Army General Zachary Taylor set up a military depot at the mouth of Brazos Santiago Pass on Brazos Island. During the war with Mexico, thousands of volunteers were encamped here, awaiting transfer to other locations. In February 1861, the U.S. Army surrendered the depot to forces of the state of Texas prior to the outbreak of the Civil War. Federal soldiers landed unopposed in 1863 at Brazos Island, taking Fort Brown and Brownsville, only to abandon them less than a year later. In May 1865, the last battle of the Civil War was fought at nearby Palmito Ranch. The depot was abandoned following hurricane damage in 1867. (1996)

Sheridan's Bridge

The line of palmetto pilings just to the north of Highway 4 at Boca Chica Beach are the remains of a Union railroad built at the close of the Civil War. These posts were the foundations of a bridge that crossed the narrow Boca Chica inlet to connect Brazos Island to the mainland at White's Ranch. When Union troops entered the Rio Grande delta in November 1863, they landed on Brazos Island and crossed the Boca Chica waterway using temporary floating pontoon bridges. After occupying Brownsville, Union general Francis Herron gave orders to build a railway and bridge that would transport troops and supplies to river steamboats that would carry them to points upriver. Union troops fell back to Brazos Island in spring 1864, scrapping plans for the line. When the Confederacy collapsed in May 1865 and Union forces re-entered Brownsville, the line again became a priority. Gen. Philip Sheridan, commander of the Union Military Division of the Southwest, feared that Confederates who had fled to Mexico might stage attacks from across the border, perhaps in alliance with Mexican Imperialist forces. Consequently, he ordered the completion of the railroad and bridge, which was constructed by US Colored Troops. The

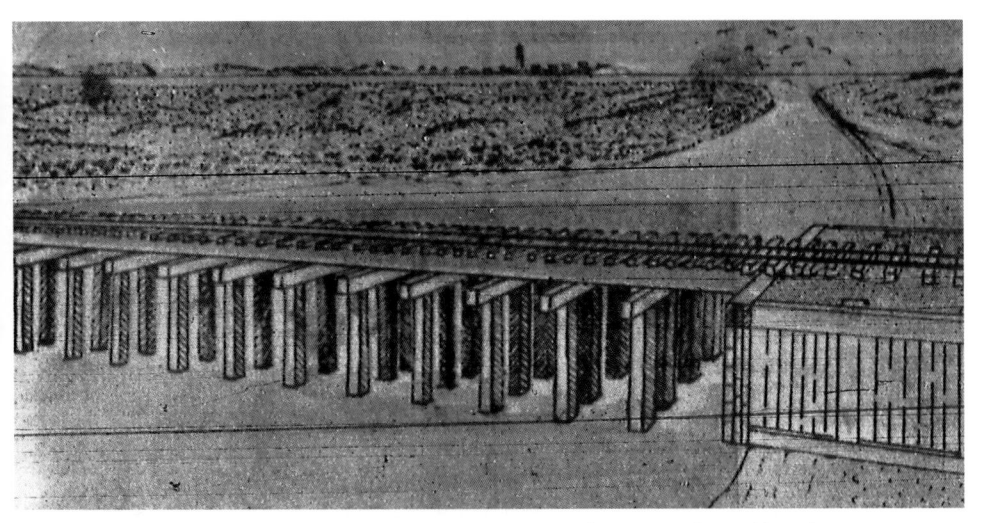

Figure 2.9. Sketch of Sheridan's Bridge recreated by Ed Valens for *Brownsville Herald* article, October 27, 1971. Courtesy of the *Brownsville Herald*.

line was a short-lived one, however: the hurricane of 1867, which wiped out the towns of Bagdad, Clarksville, and the Brazos Santiago depot, also destroyed Sheridan's Bridge. It was never rebuilt.

TEXAS HISTORICAL COMMISSION—1936 CENTENNIAL MARKER #3917
PALMETTO PILINGS
These Palmetto pilings are the remains of the Boca Chica Crossing of the Railroad from Boca Chica inlet to White's Ranch on the Rio Grande. Begun by General Francis H. Herron, USA, in 1864 and completed in 1865 by General Philip H. Sheridan for the transportation of military supplies. The Cypress piling 1,000 feet north are what remain of a floating bridge constructed across Boca Chica Inlet by General Zachary Taylor in 1846 as a part of the road from Brazos Santiago to the White Ranch Landing and Clarksville on the Rio Grande, for transportation of military supplies.

Location: Boca Chica Beach is a Texas State Park and is free and open to the public. US Highway 4 begins/ends at Boca Chica Beach. It is managed by the US Fish and Wildlife Department and is part of the Lower Rio Grande Valley National Wildlife Refuge.
GPS Coordinates: Latitude 25° 59′ 49.96″ N Longitude 97° 09′ 01.31″ W

Figure 2.10. Palmetto pilings driven in to the soft soil in 1864–65 and left behind from former Sheridan's Bridge, as seen at Boca Chica Beach in 2015.

Access: The park is always open. However, there are no facilities available for visitors. Note: When you reach the end of Highway 4 at Boca Chica Beach, turn to the left to find the pilings that remain.
Contact: None
Rio Grande Valley Civil War Trail Mobile Web: 956–847–3002;
Extension: 2015

Brownsville

Before and during the Civil War, Brownsville was a major hub in the international trade flowing out of the Rio Grande. Slavery was not common in Brownsville, so when the Civil War erupted, Brownsville residents chose sides for either personal or business reasons. When Texas seceded from the Union in February 1861, Confederates chased their Unionist neighbors out of town and confiscated their properties. Many of those Union supporters fled across the river to Matamoros and formed military units to fight their former neighbors. When Union ships blockaded the southern coastline, planters from Louisiana, Arkansas, and Texas shipped their cotton by train to the area south of Houston. From there, the "white gold" (as cotton was known) was transferred by wagons on the difficult overland journey to Brownsville, where

Figure 2.11. The War in Texas—Commerce between Brownsville and Matamoros during the Confederate occupation in 1863, *Harper's Weekly,* February 13, 1864.

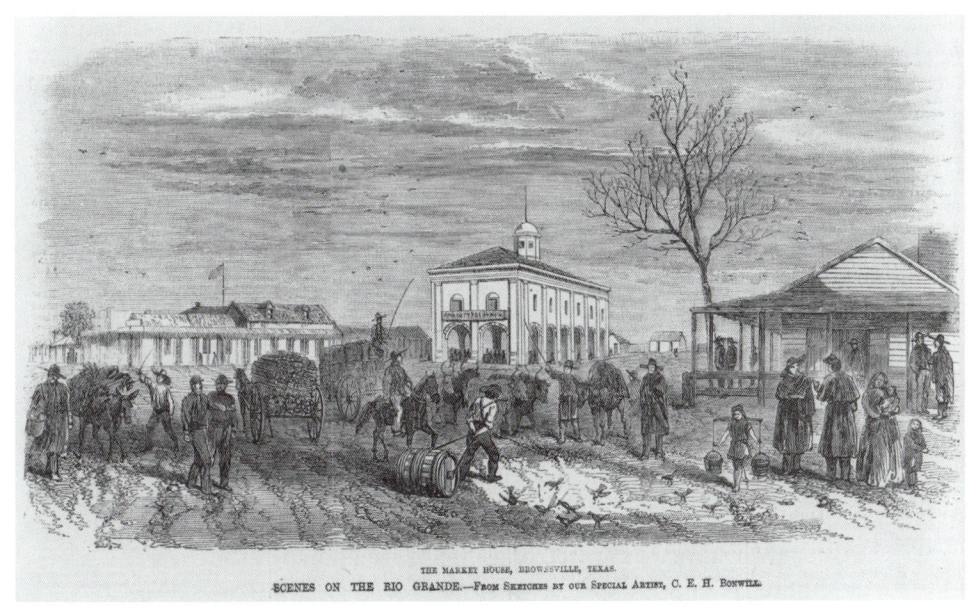

Figure 2.12. Scenes from the Rio Grande showing Market Square in Brownsville in 1864 by special artist C. E. H. Bonwill. Photograph. Retrieved from the Library of Congress, https://www.loc.gov/item/97518769/.

it could be ferried across the river to Matamoros. This was facilitated by Brig. Gen. Hamilton P. Bee, commander of the occupying Confederate forces. Mexico remained a neutral nation, so Union ships could not legally interfere with trade on the Rio Grande or in Mexican ports. By 1862, wagoneers lined up for miles along the road to Brownsville, waiting for their turn to stack their bales on the town's wharves. Hoping to stop the cotton trade, Union Army general Nathaniel P. Banks invaded South Texas in 1863. As Banks's troops burned Fort Brown and destroyed cotton awaiting export, Unionists returned from Matamoros, reclaimed their property, and this time sent the Confederates rushing to the opposite shore. Military control of the city would change two more times in 1864. In May 1865, the Confederacy surrendered, and Union forces, including US Colored Troops, reclaimed Brownsville.

Contact: None

Rio Grande Valley Civil War Trail Mobile Web: 956–847–3002; Extension: 2003

TEXAS HISTORICAL COMMISSION—MARKER #4135
PUBLIC MARKET AND TOWN HALL

Authorized 1850. On land deeded forever for this purpose. Butchers, other vendors moved in during 1851. Building complete with top story and bell tower, 1852. Town hall over market used for Presbyterian Church services. In high wind of 1867 lost its second floor. Restored 1868. Remodeled 1912, 1948. Original foundations and walls still survive in the modern market.

TEXAS HISTORICAL COMMISSION—CIVIL WAR CENTENNIAL MARKER #538
BROWNSVILLE, C.S.A.

A major center of activity for Confederacy, chief depot for war material and supplies imported from Europe through neutral port of Bagdad, Mexico. Terminus of cotton road. Point of entry and departure for important personages of South in intercourse with outside world. Occupied by large Federal expeditionary force Nov. 6, 1863, after Confederates had destroyed Ft. Brown, cotton, commissary stores and supplies and had withdrawn. Became temporary seat of Union State Government with Texan A. J. Hamilton Military Governor.

(BACK SIDE) When Confederate forces reoccupied Brownsville July 30, 1864, it resumed its importance as South's supply source and terminus of cotton road. Cotton export through Brownsville and other Rio Grande points means of survival of Confederacy west of the Mississippi. Imports from Europe and Mexico formed almost entire supply for military and civilian Gen. Magruder, Gen. Bee, Col. "Rip" Ford and other prominent Confederate officers' headquarters here. Center of international intrigue throughout the war.

Location: Market Square Research Center, 1150 Market Square, Brownsville, TX 78520
GPS Coordinates: Latitude 25° 54' 08.97" N Longitude 97° 29' 52.07" W
Access: Market Square Research Center is open by appointment to scholars, students, and amateur researchers. Tuesday through Friday: By appointment only; Saturday through Monday: Closed.
Contact: (956) 546-4242

Old City Cemetery

Although Old City Cemetery was not a military cemetery, dozens of town residents who were involved in the Civil War—either in military or governmental roles—were interred there after the war. Cotton inspector William Neale served the Confederacy militarily in Brownsville's Home Guard and in the 3rd Texas Infantry. Victor Egly was an Assistant Engineer aboard the Confederate naval ship *Neptune*. Another, Joseph James Cocke, served as a corporal in the 1st Virginia Artillery Regiment and saw action in battles at Gettysburg, Chancellorsville, and Fredericksburg. William and John Putegnat each served with units from Alabama: William in the 2nd Alabama Infantry and John in the 32nd Alabama Infantry. The graves of those who served the Union include George M. Dennett, lieutenant colonel in the 9th Regiment of US Colored Troops; Eugenio Guzman, 2nd lieutenant of the US 1st Texas Cavalry; and Welcome Alonzo Crafts, captain in the 5th New Hampshire Infantry. Many became important figures in the development of Brownsville and their names are preserved not only on the tombstones in this historic cemetery but also on schools and community buildings throughout the modern city.

TEXAS HISTORICAL COMMISSION—MARKER #539
BROWNSVILLE OLD CITY CEMETERY
Although this cemetery was not formally deeded to the City of Brownsville until 1868, dates on marked tombstones indicate the site was being used as a graveyard by the late 1850s. Buried here are some of the earliest settlers to

Figure 2.13. Old City Cemetery Center, Brownsville, Texas.

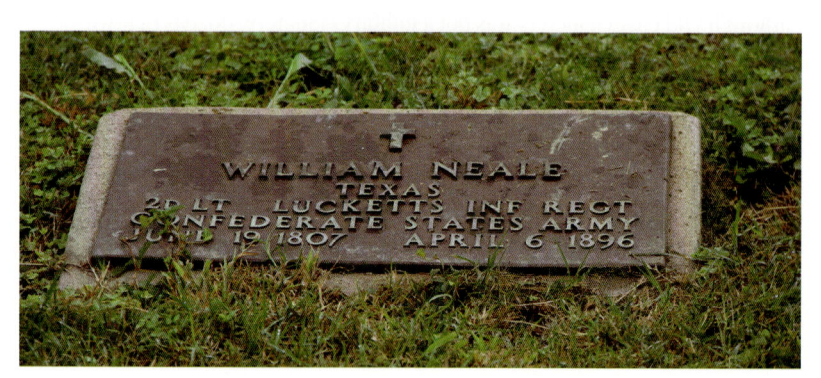

Figure 2.14. William Neale Confederate States Army grave marker, Old City Cemetery, Brownsville, Texas.

arrive in this part of the Rio Grande Valley, including the Rev. Hiram Chamberlain (1797–1866), who founded the First Presbyterian Church in Brownsville and whose daughter Henrietta married noted South Texas rancher Richard King. Others buried here include city and county government leader Joseph Webb (1850–1933), Sheriff Santiago Brito (1851–1892), first Mayor and County Judge Israel Bigelow (1811–1869), and Mexican War surgeon Charles MacManus (1824–1906). The Brownsville City Cemetery reveals much of the city's history. Victims of wars, gunfights, yellow fever, and cholera are buried here, and their graves are evidence of early conditions in the border town. The number of above-ground crypts, ornate monuments, and ironwork fences reflects the Spanish-French influence in the area. English, French, Spanish, and German tombstone inscriptions are indicative of the city's ethnic mixture. Still in use after more than one hundred years, the Brownsville City Cemetery continues to serve as a historic reminder of the region's rich heritage.

Figure 2.15. George M. Dennett US Colored Troops grave marker, Old City Cemetery, Brownsville, Texas.

Figure 2.16. 2nd Lt. Eugenio Guzman, Civil War Union Soldier buried in the Old City Cemetery, Brownsville, Texas.

HEBREW CEMETERY

Adjacent to the Old City Cemetery is the Hebrew Cemetery. Here visitors will find the grave of Louis Wise, who served in the 70th New York Infantry Regiment, and Arthur Wolff, who served as a surgeon in the Union Army.

TEXAS HISTORICAL COMMISSION—MARKER #2422
HEBREW CEMETERY

Jewish settlers came to the Brownsville/Matamoros area in the mid-1840s. In 1868, a half acre of land next to the city cemetery was purchased by the Hebrew Benevolent Society from Charles Stillman for $1. Victims of an 1858 yellow fever epidemic, who were originally buried in the city cemetery, were later reinterred here. This was the only Jewish burial ground to serve the lower Texas Valley and Matamoros until 1950. Among the many civic and business leaders buried here are immigrants from Europe and Veterans from every American War since 1845.

Location: Old City Cemetery Center, 1004 East 6th Street (Corner of 6th and Monroe), Brownsville, TX 78520
GPS Coordinates: Latitude 25° 54′ 31.21″ N Longitude 97° 30′ 01.00″ W
Access: The cemetery is open from dawn until dusk daily—Tuesday through Saturday: 10:00 a.m. to 4:00 p.m.; Sundays and Mondays: Closed.
Contact: Eugene Fernandez, Curator, Old City Cemetery and Museum, 956–541–1167

Figure 2.17. Civil War veteran Private Louis Wise grave marker, Hebrew Cemetery, Brownsville, Texas.

Charles Stillman

The historic Stillman House and its original owner, Charles Stillman, were characteristic of the Civil War era in the Rio Grande Valley. Born in Connecticut, Stillman arrived in Matamoros in 1828 and established a variety of enterprises in Northern Mexico. During the Mexican-American War, Stillman partnered with Richard King and Mifflin Kenedy to transport US troops and supplies from the Rio Grande delta to Mexico's interior. When the war ended and Mexico was forced to give up its northern territories, Stillman and his partners turned their attention to acquiring lands on the river's north bank, which he later sold for the settlement that would become Brownsville. When the Confederacy seceded from the Union, Stillman and his partners obtained a contract to transport cotton across the Rio Grande, helping Confederate growers evade the Union blockade. Stillman sent some of the cotton to his own textile factories in Monterrey. He loaded cotton onto his fleet of steamboats, which now were registered as Mexican flagged ships, and steamed them safely and legally past the warships in the gulf. Such trade prolonged the war by providing important revenue for the Confederacy. Befitting a true profiteer willing to trade with both sides, Stillman also shipped cotton into Union ports, even selling to the US government. By 1865, he had become one of the richest men in the United States. Stillman later abandoned the steamboat business and invested his money in several banks, including National City Bank of New

Figure 2.18. Home of Charles Stillman, built in 1851, still stands in Brownsville, Texas, on Washington Street in Brownsville. Courtesy of the Brownsville Heritage Museum.

Figure 2.19. Stillman House pictured here in 2016, and home of the Brownsville Heritage Museum at 1325 Washington Street in Brownsville, Texas.

York—today known as Citibank. Having made his fortune, he also left his home in Brownsville to move to New York, where he died in 1875.

> **TEXAS HISTORICAL COMMISSION—MARKER #2530**
> **HOME OF CHARLES STILLMAN**
> Home of Chas. Stillman, ship owner, merchant, rancher, who came to Brazos Santiago in 1828 and in 1849–50 founded City of Brownsville in old Espiritu Santo Land Grant. Built about 1850 for his bride, Elizabeth Goodrich, of Connecticut. Has separate kitchen, cisterns, carriage house, patio typical of pre-Civil War architecture. Recorded Texas Historic Landmark, 1964.

> **TEXAS HISTORICAL COMMISSION—1936 CENTENNIAL MARKER #2531**
> **HOME OF CHARLES STILLMAN, 1810–1875**
> Brownsville home of Charles Stillman, 1810–1875; founder of Brownsville and partner in firm of M. Kenedy and Company, which opened the Rio Grande

to steamboat navigation and controlled much of the commerce of Northern Mexico, 1848–1868. This house, erected about 1850, was the birthplace of James Stillman, President of the National City Bank of New York, 1891–1909.

Location: Brownsville Heritage Museum, Stillman House, 1325 E Washington Street, Brownsville, TX 78520
GPS Coordinates: Latitude 25° 54′ 02.81″ N Longitude 97° 29′ 47.14″ W
Access: Tuesday through Saturday: 10:00 a.m. to 4:00 p.m.; Sundays and Mondays: Closed
Admission fee: Yes (please contact site for current fee structure)
Contact: Brownsville Heritage Complex, 956-541-5560
Rio Grande Valley Civil War Trail Mobile Web: 956-847-3002; **Extension:** 2016

Neale House

One of the oldest houses still standing in Brownsville, the Neale House and its builder, William A. Neale, are both emblematic of the Civil War era in the Rio Grande Valley. Neale, an Englishman who had come to Matamoros in 1820 as a soldier of fortune during Mexico's fight for independence, established a stage line from El Fronton, now Port Isabel, to the ferry landing in Brownsville in the early 1840s. Soon afterward, he constructed a hotel, a rambling structure covering nearly a quarter of a block. Although he discontinued his stage line in 1855 and established a mercantile business twenty-five miles upriver from Brownsville at Nealeville (also called Santa Maria), he maintained interests in Brownsville, serving as the town's mayor in 1858 and 1859. During the Civil War, he served as captain of a company of home guards at Fort Brown, was a second lieutenant in the 3rd Texas Infantry Regiment, an inspector for cotton going into Mexico, and the enrolling and passport officer for Gen. Hamilton P. Bee. He witnessed naval actions of the federal blockade at the mouth of the Rio Grande and the burning of Fort Brown. When federal troops occupied Brownsville in 1863, he returned to Matamoros to live. In his absence, Union soldiers began tearing down his hotel, taking lumber to Fort Brown to build barracks. Still an English citizen, hence legally neutral in the war, Neale demanded that the general in command stop this destruction immediately. Unfortunately, only a small portion of the structure remained when removal operations ceased. That part was repaired and retained as the Neale home when he finally resettled in Brownsville in 1865.

Figure 2.20. William A. Neale House currently stands on Neale Drive just north of Ringgold Road at Texas Southmost College in Brownsville, Texas. This building was originally located at East 14th Street at Washington Street in Brownsville, near where the Stillman House stands today.

TEXAS HISTORICAL COMMISSION—MARKER #3559
NEALE HOUSE
Southern Colonial house of Wm. Neale, Englishman who was in Navy of Mexico in early 1820s, operated Matamoros to Boca Del Rio Stage Line, and lived here 1834 to 1896. Built of imported lumber. Of fine workmanship. During 1859 Cortina's War, Wm. Peter Neale, a son of the builder, was killed in right front room.

Location: Now located on Neale Drive just north of Ringgold Road at Texas Southmost College in Brownsville, Texas
GPS Coordinates: Latitude 25° 53' 37.9" N Longitude 97° 29' 41.6" W
Access: Not open to the public
Rio Grande Valley Civil War Trail Mobile Web: 956–847–3002; **Extension:** 2009
Interesting Facts: Currently the city of Brownsville owns the Neale House; however, it is scheduled to be moved to Linear Park and restored to be used by the Museum of Fine Art as either exhibit space or classrooms.

Las Rucias

On June 25, 1864, Confederate forces led by Col. John S. "Rip" Ford defeated Union troops under the command of Capt. Phillip Temple at Las Rucias. The Confederates had abandoned Brownsville in November 1863 following Union Army general Nathaniel P. Banks's invasion of South Texas, and Union soldiers advanced up the Rio Grande as far as Laredo. After their initial foray into South Texas, however, many federal troops were redeployed elsewhere, and Confederate units pushed back against the dwindling Union force. By June, Ford and his "Cavalry of the West" were within striking distance of Brownsville. Warned that Ford was nearby, Temple rode with one hundred troops of the Union 1st Texas Cavalry to the Las Rucias Ranch, about twenty-four miles west of Brownsville, hoping to take Ford's sixty-man force by surprise. But Ford had added troops from the 4th Arizona Cavalry and arrived at Las Rucias with 250 men. In a short battle, the Confederates pinned the Union troops in the ranch headquarters then routed the federals, killing twenty, wounding twenty-five, and taking thirty-six prisoners. Despite his success at Las Rucias, Ford lacked the troops and supplies to immediately follow up on his victory. By the time he was ready to strike, Union troops had already abandoned the city and the Confederates reoccupied Brownsville on July 30, 1864, without additional fighting.

Figure 2.21. Las Rucias battlefield location along US Highway 281 at the junction of Rangerville Road in front of Sacred Heart Church, San Benito, Texas.

> **TEXAS HISTORICAL COMMISSION—1936 CENTENNIAL HISTORICAL MARKER #3041**
> **LAS RUCIAS SKIRMISH**
> Colonel John S. Ford of the Confederate Army defeated the Union Forces June 25, 1864.

Location: Marker on the south side of the road in the front yard of Sacred Heart Catholic Church, 16584 US 281 (Military Highway), San Benito, Texas. At junction of Highway 281 and Rangerville Road (Farm Road 1479). Nine miles southwest of Harlingen and 1 mile north of the Rio Grande.
GPS Coordinates: Latitude 26° 03′ 13.83″ N Longitude 97° 45′ 30.30″ W
Access: Open to the public
Rio Grande Valley Civil War Trail Mobile Web: 956-847-3002; **Extension:** 2008
Interesting Facts: Some of the Union troops were from the "German" communities surrounding San Antonio. One of the survivors wrote a letter in German describing the battle, which was subsequently published by Frank Wilson Kiel et al. and titled "'Wir Waren Unser 20 Mann Gegen 150' ('We were 20 men against 150'): The Battle of Las Rucias—A Civil War Letter from a German-Texan Soldier in the 1864 Union Invasion of the Lower Rio Grande Valley." It appeared in the *Southwestern Historical Quarterly* (105, no. 3 [January 2002]: 464–78).

Palmito Ranch

Though largely unknown by the public in general, the skirmish at Palmito Ranch on May 13, 1865, was the last battle of the Civil War. Most fighting had ended after Robert E. Lee's surrender at Appomattox Court House on April 9, but many Confederate commanders west of the Mississippi had not yet accepted the Union's victory. By this time, Confederate troops still controlled Fort Brown, Brownsville, and the surrounding mainland, while a small Union garrison occupied Brazos Island. On May 11, Col. Theodore H. Barrett, commander at Brazos Island, ordered Lt. Col. David Branson to lead 250 men of the 62nd US Colored Infantry and 50 men of the 2nd Texas Cavalry toward the remaining Confederate strongholds. Branson's force advanced to Palmito Ranch and on May 13, bolstered by Barrett himself and 200 men of the 34th Indiana Infantry, pressed steadily onward toward Brownsville. The

Figure 2.22. Private John Jefferson Williams of the 34th Indiana Infantry, final battlefield fatality of the US Civil War. Courtesy of the US Army Military Institute.

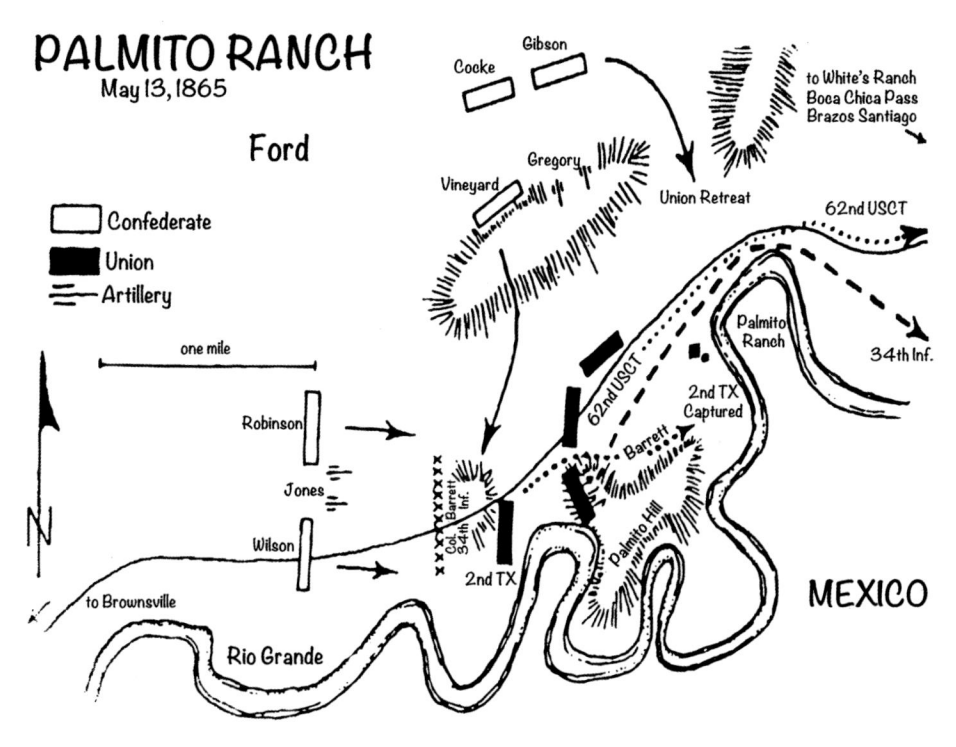

Figure 2.23. Map of Palmito Ranch Battlefield on May 13, 1865. By Elizabeth O. Skowronek adapted from https://en.wikipedia.org/wiki/Battle_of_Palmito_Ranch#/media/File:Battle_of_Palmito_Ranch_map.jpg.

Figure 2.24. Palmito Ranch Battlefield circa. 2015.

arrival of Colonel Ford with 300 Confederate cavalrymen and several artillery pieces manned by soldiers from Maximilian's army halted Barrett's advance near the western edge of Palmito Ranch. The Union infantry fell back to the coast, and as darkness fell, an artillery bombardment by Union naval ships held the Confederates at bay and allowed the federals to escape. Casualties in the battle were relatively light: the Confederates counted ten men wounded and the Union counted six wounded and two killed. One of the dead was Pvt. John Jefferson Williams of the 34th Indiana Infantry, who earned the sad distinction of becoming the final battlefield fatality in America's bloodiest war.

TEXAS HISTORICAL COMMISSION—MARKER #327
BATTLE OF PALMITO RANCH
The last land engagement of the Civil War was fought near this site on May 12–13, 1865, thirty-four days after Robert E. Lee surrendered at Appomattox. Col. Theodore H. Barrett commanded Federal troops on Brazos Island 12 miles to the east. The Confederates occupied Fort Brown 12 miles to the west, commanded by Gen. James E. Slaughter and Col. John S. (Rip) Ford, whose troops had captured Fort Brown from the Federals in 1864. Ordered to recapture the fort, Lt. Col. David Branson and 300 men advanced from Brazos Island. They won a skirmish with Confederate pickets on May 12. Barrett reinforced

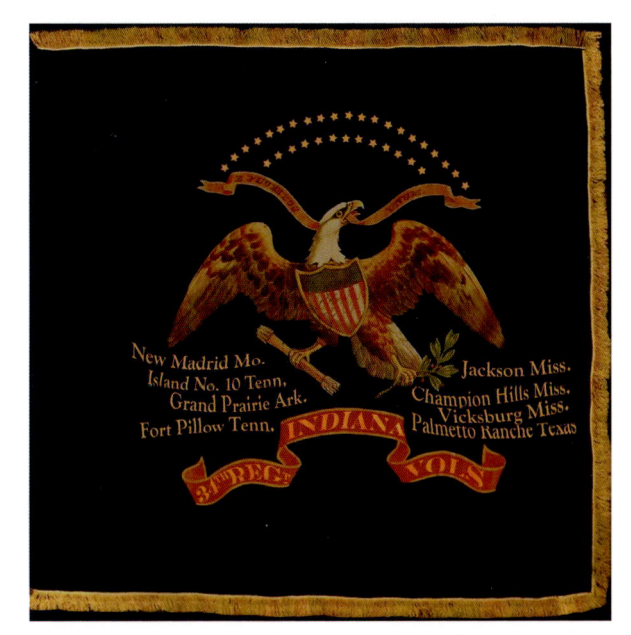

Figure 2.25. Reconstruction of the regimental flag of the US 34th Indiana Volunteers who fought at Palmito Ranch at the last battle of the US Civil War. Courtesy of Elizabeth Skowronek, based on the fragmentary original in the Indiana War Memorial Museum, Indianapolis, Indiana.

Figure 2.26. Image of a diorama depicting the Confederate cavalry charge at Palmito Ranch. Artwork courtesy of Texas Military Forces Museum, Camp Mabry, Austin, Texas, www.texasmilitaryforcesmuseum.org

Branson's troops with 200 men on May 13 and renewed the march to Fort Brown. Confederate cavalry held the Federals in check until Ford arrived with reinforcements that afternoon. Ford's artillery advanced and fired on the northern end of the Federal line while the cavalry charged. The Confederate right charged the southern end of the Federal line and captured part of the Union infantry. Barrett ordered a retreat toward the US position on Brazos Island. While the Confederates reported no fatalities in the Battle of Palmito Ranch, the Union forces reported four officers and 111 men killed, wounded or missing.

Location: 12 miles east of Brownsville on Texas Highway 4 (Boca Chica Boulevard), 43794 Palmito Hill Road, Brownsville, TX, 78521. Do not miss the wayside exhibits located just off Highway 4 on Palmito Hill Road.
GPS Coordinates: Latitude 25° 57′ 37.72″ N Longitude 97° 18′ 08.83″ W
Access: 8:00 a.m. to 5:00 p.m. No facilities are available. Administered by the US Fish and Wildlife Service.
Admission Fee: None
Rio Grande Valley Civil War Trail Mobile Web: 956–847–3002; **Extension:** 2011
Interesting Facts: Originally buried at Fort Brown, the remains of Pvt. John Jefferson Williams of the 34th Indiana Infantry were moved in 1911 to Alexandria National Cemetery in Pineville, Louisiana, where he lies in Section B, grave no. 797.

Fort Brown

As the primary US military establishment at the mouth of the Rio Grande, Fort Brown became a major prize for both sides during the Civil War. Originally named Fort Texas and later renamed in honor of Maj. Jacob Brown, one of the first casualties in the Mexican-American War, the fort was built by Gen. Zachary Taylor in 1846, making it the first major US military post built along the Rio Grande. In February 1861, Union general David Twiggs—a Southern sympathizer—agreed to surrender all military sites in Texas to the Confederacy. During most of the Civil War, Confederate troops at Fort Brown served as guardians of the prosperous cotton trade to Matamoros. In November 1863, however, Gen. Napoleon Dana and seven thousand Union troops seized control of Brownsville. However, the Union Army's presence there was brief as Union priorities shifted and troops were dispatched to other fronts.

Confederate forces under Col. John S. "Rip" Ford steadily pushed back the remaining Union troops. In July 1864, the Union once again abandoned the post, leaving Fort Brown in Southern hands for the duration of the conflict. After May 1865, Fort Brown was reoccupied by the US Army, including US Colored Troops, and became the Rio Grande district headquarters, resuming its role as a guardian of the border. Fort Brown declined in importance as Mexico stabilized following its revolutionary period (1910–17) and local law enforcement agencies replaced the military in policing the border. In September 1944 it was formally decommissioned when the 124th Cavalry was sent to Burma during World War II.

Location: 300 River Levee Road, Brownsville, TX 78523. Located just south of Texas Southernmost College and the University of Texas Rio Grande Valley Brownsville campus on Riverside Levee Drive off of University Boulevard.

GPS Coordinates: Latitude 25° 53' 46.86"N Longitude 97° 29' 18.59"W

Access: There are no facilities on-site.

Taylor's Trail Mobile Web: 956-847-3002; **Extensions:** 300, 301, 302, and 303

Rio Grande Valley Civil War Trail Mobile Web: 956-847-3002; **Extension:** 2007

Interesting Facts: Fort Brown had a military cemetery through the first decade of the twentieth century. It closed in 1909, and the bodies were reburied at Alexandria National Cemetery in Pineville, Louisiana (just outside of Alexandria). Visitors to Section B of this cemetery will find a granite marker dated 1911 erected in memory of the remains of 1,537 unknown soldiers who died at Fort Brown or at Palmito Ranch and were reinterred at Alexandria National Cemetery. Grave no. 1 at this site is to Maj. Jacob Brown, the namesake of the fort. (The cemetery website is https://www.cem.va.gov/cems/nchp/alexandriala.asp.)

Fort Brown at Texas Southmost College

Eight historic buildings associated with Fort Brown have been preserved and now serve as offices and classrooms on the campus of Texas Southmost College. These include the Commandant's Quarters (now Building No. 3), the sole remaining wooden structure, and seven other brick buildings. Most were built by the African American troops who garrisoned the post in the forty years following the American Civil War. These include the medical complex consisting of the hospital (now Gorgas Hall, Building No. 5), the Medical Laboratory (now Champion Hall, Building No. 4), the Old Morgue and linen storage building (Building No. 6), and Cavalry Hall (Building No. 28), all built in the years immediately following the Civil War. Other structures include the Post Chapel (now Regiment House, Building No. 9). Twentieth century structures include the Commissary (Art Building, Building No. 7) and the Commissary/Guardhouse/Jail (Commissary Annex, Building No. 8).

TEXAS HISTORICAL COMMISSION—MARKER #4086
POST HOSPITAL (GORGAS HALL, BUILDING NO. 5, TEXAS SOUTHMOST COLLEGE)

In March 1868, Capt. William Alonzo Wainwright arrived in Brownsville to supervise the rebuilding of Fort Brown following the Civil War and an 1867 hurricane. One of the first structures built under his direction was the Post Hospital, completed in 1869 and noted for its classical design and Palladian influences. First Lt. William C. Gorgas began studies that led to the discovery of the source of yellow fever while he was based here in 1883 (see fig. 1.13).

TEXAS HISTORICAL COMMISSION—MARKER #4087
POST HOSPITAL ANNEX

Completed in 1869 during the rebuilding of Fort Brown by Captain William Alonzo Wainwright, the Post Hospital Annex (also known as the Medical Laboratory), was constructed to house personnel assigned to work in the nearby Post Hospital. A finely crafted, classically influenced building, it subsequently was used as a medical laboratory, for storage purposes, and as a dispensary.

TEXAS HISTORICAL COMMISSION—MARKER #1964
BUILDING NOS. 85 AND 86 (OLD MORGUE, BUILDING NO. 6, AND COMMISSARY BUILDING, BUILDING NO. 7, TEXAS SOUTHMOST COLLEGE)

Morgue and linen storage. 1867 Fort Brown Buildings 85 and 86. Brick fringe, cornice. Autopsies in yellow fever study were made here by Dr. Wm. C. Gorgas, Capt. Hennessey, Lt. Crowder, Dr. Melon, defying orders of superior officer. Dr. Gorgas became immune.

Figure 2.27. Texas Southmost College map 2016, with footprint of Fort Brown superimposed. Map courtesy of Texas Southmost College, with superimposed footprint by Olga Skowronek.

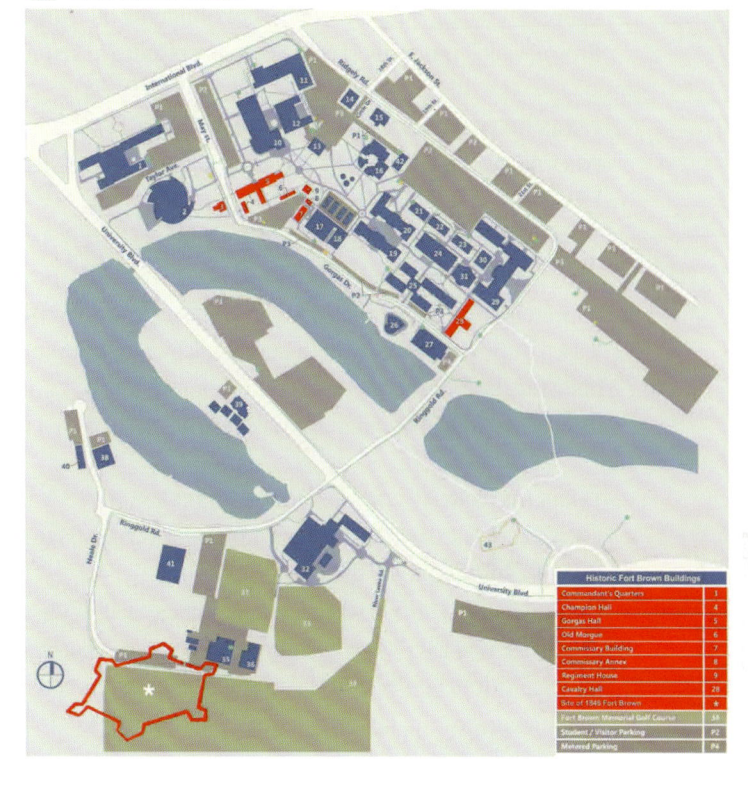

Figure 2.28. Fort Brown Post Hospital Annex built in 1869—Champion Hall of Texas Southmost College.

67

Location: The "Old Morgue" building is between the former Post Hospital (Gorgas Building) and the Commissary Building off Gorgas Drive in Fort Brown, which is now the Texas Southmost College campus.

TEXAS HISTORICAL COMMISSION—MARKER #1965
FORT BROWN CAVALRY BARRACKS (CAVALRY HALL, BUILDING NO. 28, TEXAS SOUTHMOST COLLEGE)
This building, associated with the rebuilding of Fort Brown after the Civil War, housed cavalry units until World War I, when it served as a quartermaster warehouse and commissary. Closed after World War II, the building was leased by private industry until purchased by Texas Southmost College. The one-story brick structure features an elongated T-plan, with a central entry through an arched opening, and reconstructed shed-roof porches.

TEXAS HISTORICAL COMMISSION—MARKER #1969
FORT BROWN COMMISSARY/GUARDHOUSE (COMMISSARY ANNEX, BUILDING NO. 8, TEXAS SOUTHMOST COLLEGE)
Constructed in 1905 to serve as a food storage facility, this building was abandoned one year later when Fort Brown was closed. Upon reactivation of the post during Mexican border disturbances, the building served as a guardhouse and jail. Among those quartered here were political refugees following the Battle of

Figure 2.29. Fort Brown Old Morgue on the campus of Texas Southmost College.

Figure 2.30. Fort Brown Cavalry Barracks on the campus of Texas Southmost College.

Matamoros on June 4, 1913. The structure features a loading dock and a shed roof with gabled dormer over the entrance.

Location: Historic structures associated with Fort Brown stand on the campus of the Texas Southmost College. They are located in the area bound by International Boulevard, May Street, Gorgas Drive, Ringgold Road, and Ridgely Road.
Access: The main campus is accessible to visitors at all times, though visitor access to the interiors of the buildings may require college permission.
Contact: Call the Texas Southmost College at 956–882–8200 for more information.

Bagdad

Located near the mouth of the Rio Grande, Bagdad played a vital role as a port city for Mexico and the Confederates during the Civil War. Although the ports of Texas were blockaded by Union warships, the Rio Grande was recognized as an international waterway. This allowed Mexican-flagged steamers to legally carry cotton brought into the Rio Grande Valley from other parts of Texas, Louisiana, and Arkansas to Bagdad. At times, as many as three hundred ships from England and other European nations were anchored off the coast at Bagdad, awaiting shipments of the precious fiber. Important goods such as

Figure 2.31. Fort Brown Commissary and Guardhouse on the campus of Texas Southmost College.

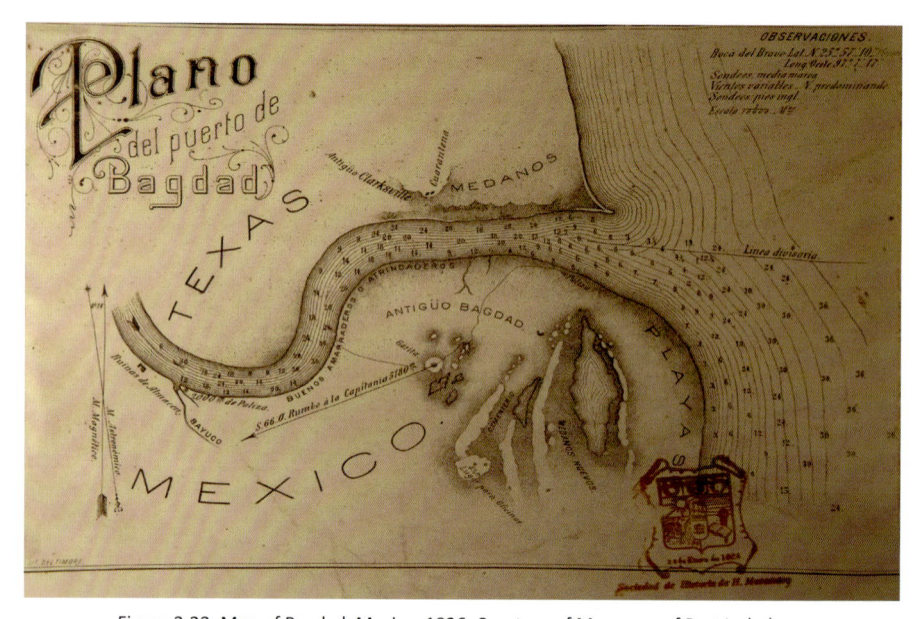

Figure 2.32. Map of Bagdad, Mexico, 1826. Courtesy of Museums of Port Isabel.

medicine, food, clothing, gunpowder, and rifles were subsequently smuggled through Bagdad as well. This small community, established in 1848, became a bustling city of twenty-five thousand inhabitants that attracted cotton brokers, sailors, teamsters, gamblers, French, Belgian, and Austrian troops in the service of Emperor Maximilian, and various assortments of criminals. When Brownsville's cotton shipments were interrupted by Union occupation in November 1863, this transport moved upriver to Laredo. The war's end quickly brought the lucrative export business of Bagdad to an end, but it was the horrific hurricane of 1867 that had the final word: Mother Nature reclaimed the once desolate, salt-sprayed sand dunes and marshland, and Bagdad now lives on only in history, tales, and memory.

TEXAS HISTORIC COMMISSION—MARKER #275
BAGDAD-MATAMOROS, C.S.A.
Civil War "Sister Cities," across the river in neutral Mexico. Were linked to Texas by a ferry which landed here. Ferry hauled to Matamoros the Confederate cotton brought from East Texas, Louisiana, Arkansas to Brownsville. In Matamoros, many speculators and agents vied for cotton to ship to Europe, via Havana. They offered in exchange vital goods: guns, ammunition, drugs, shoes, cloth. At Bagdad, on the Gulf, cotton was loaded from small boats onto ships riding the Gulf of Mexico. Goods crossing here were the South's lifeblood.

Location: South of the Rio Grande in Mexico
GPS Coordinates: Latitude 25° 56' 37.86" N Longitude 97° 08' 53.46" W
Access: None
Rio Grande Valley Civil War Trail Mobile Web: 956–847–3002; **Extension:** 2001

Clarksville
Clarksville was a small community located near the northern edge of the mouth of the Rio Grande opposite Bagdad. Founded during the 1840s, Clarksville served as a staging area for US troops during the Mexican-American War. Early in the Civil War, Clarksville prospered because of the cotton trade and presence of Confederate blockade runners. In 1863, however, the area was captured and occupied by Union forces, which seized private homes and warehouses and caused most residents to flee. As part of Emperor Maximilian's

efforts to suppress Mexican resistance, French gunboats occasionally shelled Clarksville. Theresa Clark Clearwater, daughter of the town's founder, recalled that "often the families were forced to take refuge behind some big sand hill during these bombardments." Troops of the Texas Confederate cavalry, as well as French and Austrian soldiers from Maximilian's forces, also frequented Clarksville. In 1866, American filibusters, private soldiers of fortune, attacked Maximilian's Imperial forces at neighboring Bagdad with the help of black soldiers from the 118th US Colored Infantry. The great hurricane of 1867 killed many residents and caused heavy damage to Clarksville, but the community survived. In 1872, the building of a railway from Brownsville to Port Isabel diverted commerce away from Clarksville, which was damaged again by storms in 1874 and 1886. Eventually, the little community ceased to exist, and a change in the course of the Rio Grande in 1953 resulted in the river flowing over the old site.

Location: Site destroyed
GPS Coordinates: Latitude 25° 57′ 15.64″ N Longitude 97° 09′ 05.54″ W
Access: None
Rio Grande Valley Civil War Trail Mobile Web: 956–847–3002; **Extension:** 2004

Figure 2.33. Engraving of a bustling Bagdad, Mexico, and an armada of ships in the Gulf of Mexico. Carte de Visite engraving by unknown artist, 1864–65. Courtesy of Brownsville Historical Association.

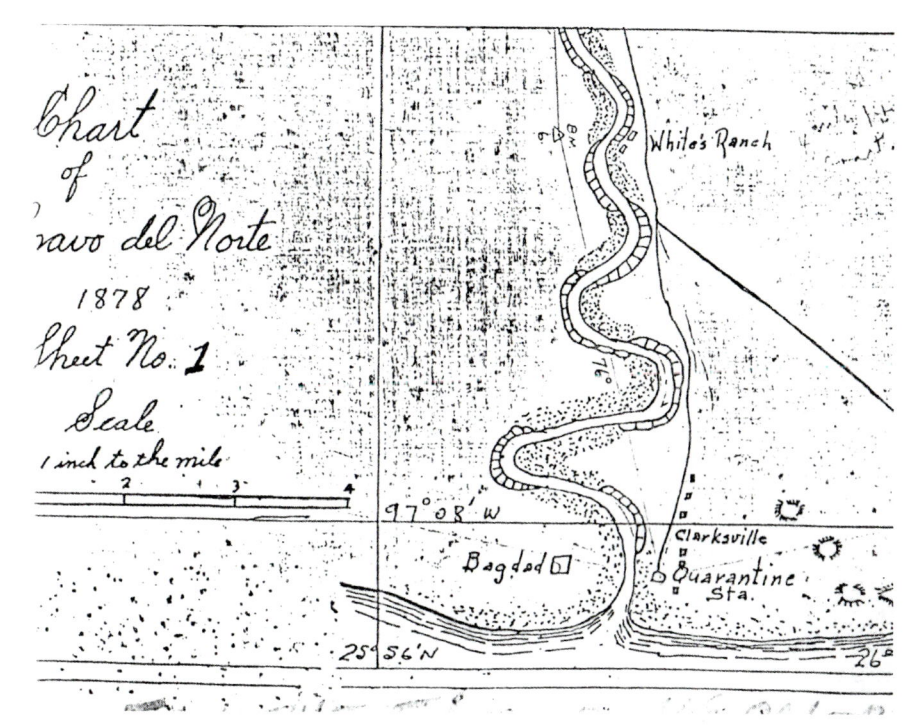

Figure 2.34. 1878 Map of sister towns of Bagdad, Mexico, and Clarksville, Texas. Courtesy of the McCaleb files at University of Texas Rio Grande Valley Special Collection Archives.

Point Isabel

Formerly known as El Fronton, Point Isabel had been a major commercial center before the Civil War era. Its significance was marked in 1852 by the construction of a major lighthouse to guide ships through the Brazos Santiago pass, the tallest structure in the vicinity. Although the town declined in importance after steam technology made safe passage directly into the Rio Grande possible, the lighthouse served as a beacon for small Confederate trade ships that used the port to avoid the Union blockade. When Union troops occupied South Texas in 1863, the Confederates attempted to blow up the lighthouse to prevent it from being used as an enemy observation post, but their efforts failed: they only damaged the top part. When Confederates recaptured the Rio Grande Valley in the summer of 1864, they pushed the Union troops back to Brazos Island and kept a close watch from the nearby point to guard against an amphibious landing. The most significant clash between the two forces came on August 9 at the Point Isabel docks when 250 Confederate cavalrymen skirmished with 75 men of the Corps of African Engineers—a unit of black freedmen from Louisiana. In March 1865, US general Lew Wallace, who later gained fame as a governor of the New Mexico territory and author of the bestselling historical novel *Ben Hur*, met here with rebel leaders James E. Slaughter and John S. "Rip" Ford to discuss a cease fire for the Rio Grande delta. Although they reached no formal arrangement, they did agree to an informal truce, which lasted until hostilities again broke out at Palmito Ranch.

Rio Grande Valley Civil War Trail Mobile Web: 956–847–3002; **Extension:** 2013

Port Isabel Historical Museum

Visitors following the Rio Grande Valley Civil War Trail should begin their visit at the Port Isabel Historical Museum. Here you will find exhibits and artifacts from the Mexican-American War to present.

Location: 317 East Railroad Avenue, Port Isabel, TX 78578.
GPS Coordinates: Latitude 26° 04′ 39.66″ N Longitude 97° 12′ 27.16″ W
Access: Hours: Tuesday through Saturday: 10 a.m. to 4p.m.; Sunday and Monday: Closed
Admission fee: Yes (please contact site for current fee structure)
Contact: 956–943–7602

Figure 2.35. Treasures of the Gulf Museum. Formerly a store owned by Charles Champion. Courtesy of Museums of Port Isabel.

Figure 2.36. Artifacts discovered at Bagdad Beach. Courtesy of Museums of Port Isabel.

TEXAS HISTORICAL COMMISSION—MARKER #4796
FORT POLK

A Mexican village developed on this point, settled by Mexican ranchers in the 1700's. The village was abandoned prior to the US Declaration of war with Mexico in 1846. US Forces led by General Zachary Taylor occupied the point on March 24, 1846. Taylor erected a depot here to receive supplies from New Orleans. The six-sided Fort, named for President Polk, consisted of 4 sides of Earthen Embankments and 2 sides open to the shoreline. The Fort was abandoned in 1850 but the settlement it attracted eventually developed into Port Isabel. Remnants of the Fort were visible until the 1920s.

Taylor's Trail Mobile Web: 956–847–3002; **Extensions:** 500 and 501

TEXAS HISTORICAL COMMISSION—1936 CENTENNIAL MARKER #3780
OLD POINT ISABEL LIGHTHOUSE

The beacon for the commerce of the Rio Grande; Erected by the United States Government in 1852; Extinguished during the Civil War; Discontinued, 1888–1895; Permanently discontinued, 1905.

Taylor's Trail Mobile Web: 956–847–3002; **Extension:** 502

Figure 2.37. Point Isabel Light Station. Artist unknown. Courtesy of Museums of Port Isabel.

Figure 2.38. Port Isabel Lighthouse, State Historical Site 2017. Courtesy of Museums of Port Isabel.

TEXAS HISTORICAL COMMISSION—MARKER #4063
POINT ISABEL, C.S.A.

After Texas seceded and joined the Confederacy, the Federal Navy in late 1861 blockaded this port with the US "Santiago de Cuba." Commerce stoppage caused removal of customs offices to Brownsville and some civilians to neutral Bagdad, Mexico. The Confederates ceased to use the lighthouse, and it became a watch tower for blockade runners, and thus Laguna Madre their haven. Boats from the U.S.S. Brooklyn, in May 1863, attacked vessels in port and a Confederate unit near the lighthouse. The Confederates tried to blow up the tower—a defense measure—but only succeeded in damaging fixtures. The French, supporting Maximilian in Mexico, prohibited the landing of war material at Bagdad. Defying both the French and US Naval patrols, Mexican lighters from the Rio Grande landed here in September 1863 with a large cargo of C.S.A. arms. In Nov. 1863, US forces from the expedition of Gen. N.P. Banks occupied Point Isabel. The blockade was lifted and the port reactivated. In August 1864, the Confederates drove the Federals across the bay to Brazos Island. The next March, Federal Gen. Lew Wallace (later author of *Ben Hur*) met Confederate officers here to talk peace.

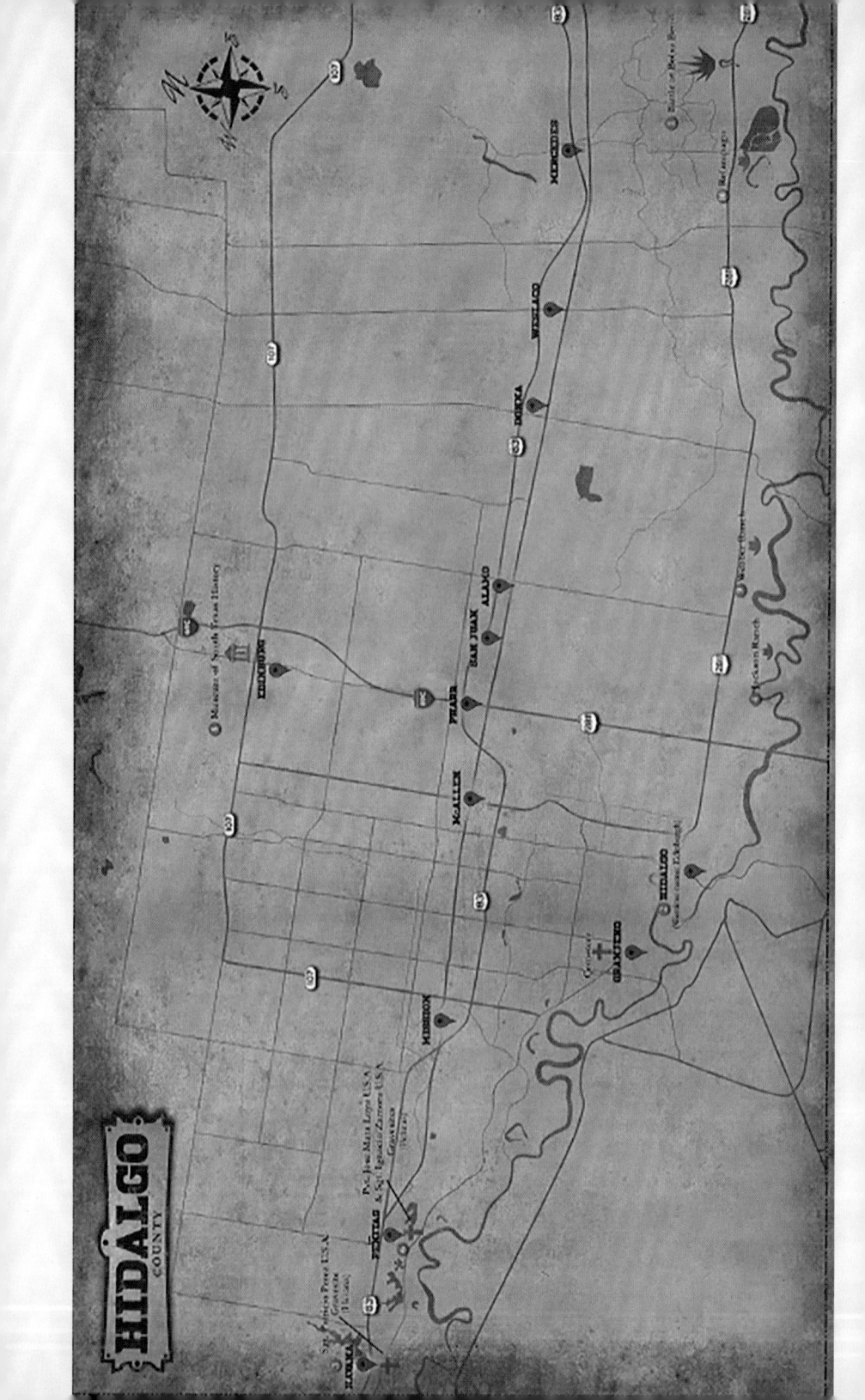

HIDALGO COUNTY

3

Hidalgo County Sites and Events

Visitors exploring the Rio Grande Valley Civil War Trail will traverse Hidalgo County in South Texas. Today this county is bordered by Cameron County on the east, Brooks County on the north, Starr County on the west, and the Rio Grande and Mexico to the south. Nonaboriginal peoples from Monterrey first settled in the area in the second half of the eighteenth and first two decades of the nineteenth centuries. As a result, the area was incorporated into the viceroyalty of New Spain as a part of Nuevo Santander. Reynosa and other communities including Mier and Camargo were founded around 1749 on the south side of the Rio Grande. Settlers in those communities received long narrow land grants that bordered the Rio Grande in Hidalgo County by the Spanish and later Mexican governments. Known as *porciónes*, cattle and sheep ranches were established in the largely waterless interior of these grants while subsistence agriculture was practiced along the margins of the Rio Grande.

A quarter of a century later, in 1774 the first settlement called *La Habitación*, also known as *Rancho San Luis* or *San Luisito*, was founded north of the river at the site of present-day Hidalgo, Texas. Two dozen years later in the 1790s, larger interior land grants, including the Santa Anita grant (known today as the McAllen Ranch), came into being.

Following Mexican independence in 1821, the region was administered for the next quarter of a century as a part of the State of Coahuila y Texas. Contrary to the wishes of the Republic of Texas following independence in 1836, the region south of the Nueces River, which included the future Hidalgo County, remained a part of the Republic of Mexico until the signing of the Treaty of Guadalupe Hidalgo in 1848, ending the Mexican-American War and establishing the Rio Grande and the international boundary between the two republics.

Hidalgo County was formed in 1852 and named for Miguel Hidalgo y Costilla, whose cry for independence in 1810 sparked the Mexican independence movement. At this time, the county had more than forty ranches. La Habitación was renamed Edinburgh and made county seat. The first county court convened on September 2, 1852, and as its first act issued licenses to ferries at Hidalgo, San Luis, Peñitas, and Las Cuevas.

According to the 1860 census, there were 190 farms in Hidalgo County and 54 percent of some 1,200 enumerated individual residents were born outside of the county. Ninety-eight percent were listed as "white," with the remaining 2 percent classified as "nonwhite." Many of the former were Mexican American descendants of the original settlers who had arrived in the eighteenth century. During the American Civil War, some like Patricio Pérez of Havana and Ignacio Zamora of Peñitas remained loyal to the Union and served in the 2nd Regiment of the Texas Cavalry. Others served with the Confederacy. Often their choice of sides was based on their role in earlier conflicts such as the Cortina War, which pitted various local elites against one another in the decade following the annexation of the region from Mexico. Bolsa Bend in El Zacatal, south of Progreso in southeast Hidalgo County, was the site of one of these battles in 1860.

As a part of the United States, there was an influx of new people into the county. Some like John Young and John McAllen (see fig. 1.4), who originated in the British Isles, would marry into local Mexican American families following service in the US Army during the Mexican-American War. Others like the Webbers, Jacksons, Rutledges, and Singleterrys arrived from the United States with their formerly enslaved African American wives. This was an attractive corner of the United States for interracial marital unions of this kind, which were outlawed elsewhere. Because this region was formerly part of Mexico, many of the laws and customs associated with Mexico were still recognized. Mexico had outlawed slavery decades earlier, and interracial marriage was a common aspect of life under colonial Spain and the Republic. Here, far from the prejudice which characterized antebellum America, these individuals were able to live freely as families ranching, farming, and operating ferries along the Rio Grande. A southern branch of the Underground Railroad ran through these farming ranches to the ferries (*chalons*) of the Rio Grande and from there to the safety of Mexico. Members of these families served in the Union Army, but after the Civil War some of the children of the founding interracial couples married Confederate veterans.

During the American Civil War, Mexico served as a haven for both Confederate and Union sympathizers. Mexican President Benito Juárez supported Abraham Lincoln and the Union. To this day, in the region a number of public schools are named "Juárez-Lincoln," commemorating this alliance. The fluidity of the border during the Civil War is underscored by a raid led by Octaviano Zapata, who with some seventy compatriots crossed the Rio Grande from Mexico on December 28, 1862, at Los Ebanos and later in Starr County captured a Confederate wagon train killing three teamsters in the melee. This was at a time when the troops of Napoleon III were fighting the armies of President Juárez. The following year they would turn over Mexico to the newly arrived Austrian-born Mexican Emperor Maximilian of Habsburg, who was friendly with the Confederacy. Following the end of the war and until the fall of Mexican Emperor Maximilian in 1867, US Colored Troops were stationed in Hidalgo to forestall Confederate sympathizers from crossing into Imperial Mexico.

Those traveling the Rio Grande Valley Civil War Trail should first orient themselves in the region's history at the Museum of South Texas History in Edinburg.

Museum of South Texas History

The Museum of South Texas History (located on the north side of Edinburg's Courthouse Square) is accredited by the American Alliance of Museums. Founded in 1967 in the 1910 Hidalgo County Jail as the Hidalgo County Historical Museum, it preserves and presents the borderland heritage of South Texas and Northeastern Mexico through its permanent collections, archives, and exhibits spanning prehistory through the twentieth century. Its collections include significant holdings relating to the era of the American Civil War, including sabers, carbines, and other weapons and other objects from the Palmito Ranch battle, Bagdad, and Brazos Santiago. Of special interest to visitors exploring the Rio Grande Valley Civil War Trail is a life-sized replica of a portion of the steamboat *Mustang*. That portion of the gallery deals with the role of Rio Grande steamboats in the Civil War cotton trade.

Location: The Museum of South Texas History is located at 200 N Closner Boulevard, Edinburg, TX 78541. It is open to the public every day except

Figure 3.1. Museum of South Texas History and their river highway exhibit of steamboat *Mustang*.

Mondays and major national holidays. Allow a minimum of an hour and a half for your visit.
GPS Coordinates: Latitude 28° 18′ 08.78″ N Longitude 98° 09′ 41.59″ W
Admission Fee: Yes (please contact site for current fee structure)
Contact: 956–383–6911
Rio Grande Valley Civil War Trail Mobile Web: 956–847–3002; **Extension:** 2209

Salt Lakes

In the era of the American Civil War, salt was a strategic resource. It was essential for tanning leather, preserving foods, and for maintaining the health of livestock and people. Texas had a number of salt works that provided this mineral to the Confederacy. These included the Palestine salt works in Anderson County north of Houston; the Ledbetter salt works in Shackelford County west of Fort Worth near Abilene; and the Lometa salt works near Austin in Lampasas County. Producing salt at these sites was a labor-intensive process requiring the cutting and burning of wood to evaporate water and thus precipitate salt crystals from a hyper saline solution. In Deep South Texas there are three salt lakes in Hidalgo and Willacy counties: La Sal del Rey, La Sal Vieja, and La Sal Blanca. Here, where there is an annual deficit of rainfall, salt crystals precipitate during dry periods and can be easily gathered by hand without the laborious boiling process.

La Sal del Rey

For centuries, this remote site was a destination for American Indians, Spanish settlers, Mexican traders, and Anglo-Americans who sought the rich source of valuable white crystals known as salt. La Sal del Rey is the site of a large salt lake and was South Texas' main source of vital salt during the Civil War. In addition to seasoning, salt was the chief means of preserving meat and fish. Livestock, including cattle, mules, and horses needed it, and the white crystals were used in curing leather for shoes, harnesses, and other military goods. Wagon loads of salt went south to Brownsville for shipment from Matamoros and Bagdad. Empty cotton wagons returning from Brownsville often stopped here to load salt for destinations in Central and East Texas. In 1863, Union forces destroyed the salt works. The following year, when Confederates took control of the Valley again, they used La Sal del Rey as a staging point and re-

Figure 3.2. Present-day image of Sal del Rey, northern Hidalgo County.

opened the mines. The name La Sal del Rey is Spanish, meaning "The King's Salt," a reference to royal ownership of valued mineral sources in colonial times. After the Civil War, a legal controversy over the lake's ownership led to the State of Texas declaring that mineral rights belonged to private property owners and not to the general public. Salt mining continued at La Sal del Rey until the 1940s. Today it is a nature preserve, looking much as it did during the 1860s.

TEXAS HISTORICAL COMMISSION—HISTORICAL MARKER #1441
EL SAL DEL REY (THE SALT OF THE KING)
Directly to the north. Upon Spanish discovery, 1746, claimed for King, under old law that salt was money. People of wide area got salt here. 1863–64 works aided Texas in the Civil War. Later disputes over El Sal del Rey established Texas laws for private ownership of minerals. (1964)

TEXAS HISTORICAL COMMISSION—CIVIL WAR MEMORIAL HISTORICAL MARKER #1442
EL SAL DEL REY, C.S.A.
Large salt lake located 26 miles northeast was principal source of salt in South Texas during the Civil War. Put under state guard and agent 1862. Salt sold to families, Texas Military Board, Army of Confederacy and wagons returning north on cotton road-vital trade route for South thru Mexico. Due to military and domestic importance, Union forces periodically wrecked the salt works from November 1863 until war's end. It was also a Texas Confederate base for the 1864 recapture of Brownsville. A memorial to Texas who served the Confederacy; erected by the State of Texas 1963. Back side: Salting or smoking were used to preserve meat at time of Civil War. When South levied a meat tithe, salt necessary to cure bacon and beef for military. Salt was a must for horses and mules used by cavalry, artillery and supply wagons. Hides were preserved with it to make leather for shoes and harness. Other wartime salt works were operated along coast and in 7 counties in central, east and west Texas. El Sal del Rey, Spanish for "Salt for the King" also played a significant role in the history of Texas mineral law. A legal controversy raged for years over its ownership. Under Spain, mineral rights belonged to crown. Mexico retained the principle of the state ownership of minerals. Texas, as Republic and State,

kept minerals in the public domain. Private possession of the lake began with the 1866 Texas Constitutional Convention which relinquished all minerals to landowners. The principle of private ownership was readopted in the Constitutions of 1869 and 1876.

Location: From Edinburg, visitors should travel 20 miles north on US 281/I 69 C and exit eastbound on US 186. Then travel 4 miles. An information kiosk and trail to the salt lake and flats is located on the north side of the road, and the historical marker is located another half a mile east, also on the north side of Highway 186. From Harlingen, go north on Highway 77 for about 24 miles. Exit 186 West for approximately 22 miles to the kiosk. For more information, tune into AM 530.
GPS Coordinates: Latitude 26° 31′ 26.13″ N Longitude 98° 04′ 42.07″ W
Access: La Sal del Rey is a unit of the Lower Rio Grande Valley National Wildlife Refuge and is administered by the US Fish and Wildlife Service. There are no facilities on-site. Wear sturdy walking shoes; bring insect repellent, sunscreen, a hat, and water.
Rio Grande Valley Civil War Trail Mobile Web: 956–847–3002; **Extension:** 2206

McAllen Ranch

West of the salt lakes was Rancho Santa Anita, known today as the McAllen Ranch. In the 1860s, the Rancho Santa Anita, owned by Irish merchant and stockman John McAllen, was one of many ranches in Hidalgo County. The presence of water wells made it a natural magnet for freighters, travelers, and soldiers. McAllen had mercantile operations in Matamoros, Brownsville, and historic Edinburgh, now called Hidalgo. A British citizen, he declared himself neutral in the Civil War. McAllen, his son James, and his stepson John Young supplied beef, hides, and tallow to Confederate and Union forces alike. During the Valley's Union occupation in 1863 and 1864, cavalry troops from Fort Brown camped at various spots on his Santa Anita ranch. From camps here and at other nearby sites, federal troops searched for enemy patrols and tried to disrupt the wagon trains carrying cotton and salt. During the Civil War, ranchers with known Confederate sympathies often found their properties raided and burned, but due to its owners' neutral stance, the Santa Anita was not among those destroyed.

TEXAS HISTORICAL COMMISSION—HISTORICAL MARKER #13559
MCALLEN RANCH
The McAllen Ranch has historic ties to Spanish Texas, when this region was part of Nuevo Santander, a colonial area founded by José de Escandón along the lower Rio Grande. In 1790, José Manuel Gómez of Reynosa and Moncolova received the vast (95,000 acres) Santa Anita land grant. He built fences, worker housing, water wells at San Juanito and Santa Anita, and raised cattle, sheep, goats and horses. He wed Gregoria Ballí Domínguez, a widow with two sons, who inherited the majority of the Santa Anita. A niece, María Salomé Ballí de la Garza, also came to acquire a share of the grant. In 1848, Salomé married Matamoros merchant John Young, and they bought remaining portions of the Gómez grant, as well as additional land. Upon Young's death in 1859, Salomé managed the estate with Young's associate, Irishman John McAllen, whom she wed in 1861 (see fig. 1.4). They bought remaining rights in the Santa Anita, reuniting the grant. Salomé's sons, John J. Young and James Ballí McAllen, worked with John McAllen to operate the ranch, which supplied beef, tallow, hides and refuge to both Confederate and Union troops during the Civil War. At one time, the family managed more than 160,000 acres. Upon Salomé's death in 1898, the two half-brothers divided the land, with Young inheriting the eastern Santa Anita portion and McAllen the western San Juanito portion, which he ran with his father as the McAllen Ranch under the SM (for Salomé Ballí McAllen) brand. James died in 1916, leaving the ranch to his widow, Margaret, and their four children. They and their descendants continued operating the ranch, which received honors as one of the oldest Texas ranches in continuous operation by the same family. (2006)

Location: Rancho Santa Anita, the McAllen ranch lies 20 miles north of Edinburg. It is located on Highway 1017 west of Linn / San Manuel, in Hidalgo County.
GPS Coordinates: Latitude 26° 34′ 39.44″ N Longitude 98° 10′ 29.04″ W
Access: Privately owned, working ranch. Not open to the public. Texas historical marker on Highway 1017, 13 miles west of Linn, gives the ranch history.
Rio Grande Valley Civil War Trail Mobile Web: 956–847–3002; **Extension:** 2208

City of Hidalgo (Civil War Era Name: Edinburgh)

Founded in 1774 as La Habitación, and also known as Rancho San Luis or San Luisito, by the 1850s, this ranching settlement on the Rio Grande had become an important crossing point between the United States and Mexico. Later renamed Edinburgh, it had a mercantile store, along with a ferry and steamboat landing. Located across the Rio Grande from Reynosa, Mexico, and roughly halfway between Fort Brown and Ringgold Barracks, the town became a strategic objective for Union and Confederate forces during the Civil War. It was founded at the site of a Rio Grande ferry crossing on the "salt trail," which ran from La Sal del Rey to northern and central Mexico. In 1848, in accordance with the Treaty of Guadalupe Hidalgo, the village became part of the United States. A Scottish merchant named John Young opened a store here in 1852. Despite its Spanish and Mexican name and culture, Young renamed the settlement Edinburgh after his home city in Scotland. With a ferry crossing the river and a steamboat landing, Edinburgh grew in population and military importance. The Military Highway between Forts Brown and Ringgold ran nearby. During the Civil War, Edinburgh passed back and forth between Union and Confederate control. When Union forces occupied Brownsville in late 1863, the main Confederate cotton trail to Mexico shifted upriver to Edinburgh, and

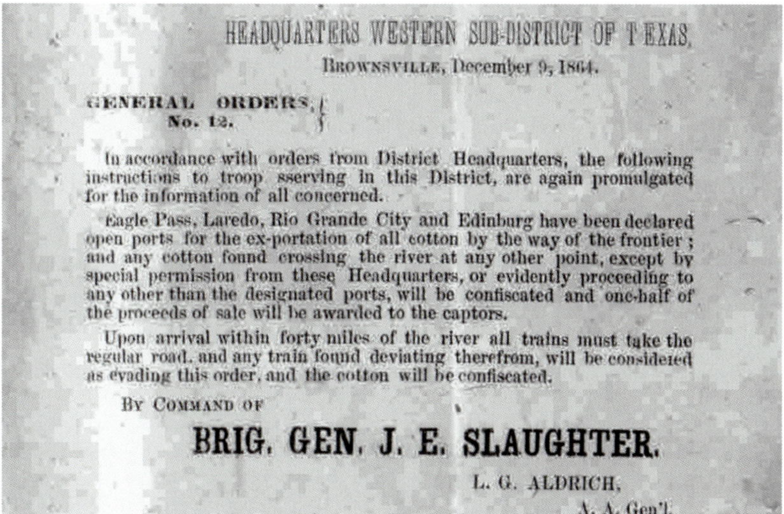

HEADQUARTERS WESTERN SUB-DISTRICT OF TEXAS,
BROWNSVILLE, December 9, 1864.

GENERAL ORDERS, No. 12.

In accordance with orders from District Headquarters, the following instructions to troop sserving in this District, are again promulgated for the information of all concerned.

Eagle Pass, Laredo, Rio Grande City and Edinburg have been declared open ports for the ex-portation of all cotton by the way of the frontier; and any cotton found crossing the river at any other point, except by special permission from these Headquarters, or evidently proceeding to any other than the designated ports, will be confiscated and one-half of the proceeds of sale will be awarded to the captors.

Upon arrival within forty miles of the river all trains must take the regular road, and any train found deviating therefrom, will be considered as evading this order, and the cotton will be confiscated.

BY COMMAND OF

BRIG. GEN. J. E. SLAUGHTER.

L. G. ALDRICH,
A. A. Gen'l.

Figure 3.3. Confederate Brig. Gen. James E. Slaughter's orders declaring Edinburg, among other towns, as open ports for exportation of cotton along the frontier. Courtesy of the University of Texas Rio Grande Valley Special Collections Archive.

from here the cotton wagon trains headed farther west to Rio Grande City and Laredo. After July 1864, Confederate forces regained control of the town and crossing, and held it until the war ended in May 1865. At that time, Edinburgh was occupied by Union forces, including US Colored Troops. It was renamed Hidalgo in 1885.

In Hidalgo County the largest concentration of National Register of Historic Places structures dating from the closing decades of the nineteenth century may be found in the city of Hidalgo the original county seat. Visitors to the town will want to visit the newly restored nineteenth century courthouse and the 1910 Old Hidalgo Pumphouse, a World Birding Center, located at 902 S. Second Street in Street, Hidalgo, Texas TX 78557 (956–843–8686), is open Monday through Friday: 10:00 a.m. to 5:00 p.m.; Saturday: Closed; Sunday: 1:00 p.m. to 5:00 p.m.

TEXAS HISTORICAL COMMISSION—1936 CENTENNIAL HISTORICAL MARKER #5530

TOWN OF HIDALGO

County seat of Hidalgo County 1854–1908. Known as Edinburgh in 1852. Name changed in 1861 to Hidalgo in honor of Miguel Hidalgo y Costilla, 1753–1811, parish priest who led the movement in 1810 for Mexican independence. Almost completely washed away by an overflow of the Rio Grande in September, 1887.

Hidalgo, Texas

Location: Located on the Rio Grande, about 8 miles south of McAllen, Texas
GPS Coordinates: Latitude 26° 05′ 57.74″ N Longitude 98° 15′ 45.80″ W
Access: The city's oldest section, or historic district, is presumed to be accessible by private vehicles at any time or day. Border security conditions may inhibit access to locations directly adjacent to the river itself, such as levees.
Rio Grande Valley Civil War Trail Mobile Web: 956–847–3002; **Extension:** 2203

Havana

Located between La Joya and Sullivan City on US 83 North, Havana was one of many ranchos along the Military Highway. Founded in 1767, Havana was named for the Cuban capital and port city. When the Civil War began, Havana was caught up in the sectional conflict. Generations of vaqueros and workers were born on the ranch and lived here. Among them was Patricio Pérez, who like most vaqueros was a skilled horseman. After Texas left the United States in 1861, many Tejanos put their equestrian skills to use by joining the Confederate cavalry. But Patricio Pérez remained loyal to the Union. When federal troops occupied the Valley in late 1863, Pérez rode to Brownsville, where he enlisted with the 2nd Regiment of the Texas Cavalry, one of nearly a thousand Tejanos to join Texas' federal forces. He was issued the standard uniform, saber, and revolver, but a wartime photo shows him holding a big sombrero instead of regular army headgear. Pérez earned the rank of sergeant in 1864. The 2nd Regiment saw duty in the Brownsville area until it was ordered to New Orleans in July 1864. It remained in Louisiana and Mississippi until the war ended. Its soldiers, Sergeant Pérez among them, mustered out in November 1865. Patricio Pérez returned to Havana and to his life as a vaquero and rancher. He died in his seventies in 1908, and is buried in the town's cemetery, with his wife Martina resting beside him.

Figure 3.4. Union soldier 1st Sgt. Patricio Pérez, 2nd Texas Cavalry from Havana Ranch. Courtesy of Delia Alaniz.

Hidalgo County Sites and Events

Location: Cemetery is located on the south side of US 83, about 1.8 miles west of La Joya, in the community of Havana. Those traveling US Highway 83 will cross "Patricio Pérez" Road, which was named for the veteran. Open at all times.
GPS Coordinates: Latitude 26° 14′ 51.35″ N Longitude 98° 30′ 27.47″ W
Rio Grande Valley Civil War Trail Mobile Web: 956–847–3002; **Extension:** 2204

Peñitas Cemetery

Three miles east of Havana in Peñitas is the final resting place of two local Union Army veterans: Pvt. José María Loya and Sgt. Ignacio Zamora. Private Loya enlisted in the Independent Partisan Rangers, Texas Cavalry, in November 1863. Zamora enlisted in the 2nd Regiment, Texas Cavalry Company, at Brownsville in 1864. Both descended from Spanish colonial families who founded the settlement called Peñitas in the mid-1700s, which then—like all of Texas—was part of New Spain, and after 1821, the Republic of Mexico. After the Mexican-American War ended in 1848, the Mexican government was forced to recognize the Rio Grande as an international boundary. People of Mexican origin whose homes lay north of the boundary often became targets of land theft and violence. This may have inspired them to join the Union Army as a form of retaliation against their Confederate neighbors. Many willingly went to Brownsville to enlist into local regiments, such as the 2nd Regiment of the Texas Cavalry, in fear of being conscripted and sent far away. It is also noted that bounty money was offered to enlist in the Union Army. This appealed to some local vaqueros who were not only opposed to slavery but as ranchers and farmers were dealing with the loss of family land grant properties at the end of the Mexican-American War.

Visitors to the grave of Ignacio Zamora should note that his descendants were so proud of his service in the Union Army that they added an additional horizontal marker engraved "Civil War Vet Union."
Location: The city of Peñitas is located between the city of Palmview and the city of La Joya. Driving west on US 83, about 16 miles from McAllen, turn south on FM 1427 (also known as Main Street). After about 1 mile, turn left on Zamora Street, which is immediately after the Peñitas Public Library. If you reach the railroad tracks, you have gone too far. Drive about a quarter of a mile down Zamora Street (which will eventually curve to the right), and turn left on

Figure 3.5. Peñitas Cemetery gravestones of Tejano Union Soldiers Sgt. Ignacio Zamora and Pvt. José María Loya. Private Loya originally went to Brownsville in November of 1863 to enlist in the Confederate Cavalry as they were recruiting skilled horsemen at Fort Brown. However, by the time he arrived, the Union Army was in control of the area, so he enlisted in the Union Cavalry instead.

Manuelita Rios Street, which is the first street that crosses Zamora Street. You will see the Peñitas Cemetery to your left.
GPS Coordinates: Latitude 26° 13′ 39.80″ N Longitude 98° 26′ 35.46″ W
Access: The Peñitas Cemetery is open 24 hours a day, 7 days a week.
Contact: Peñitas Public Library (956–583–5658), at 1111 S. Main Street, Peñitas, TX 78576. Monday through Thursday: 9:00 a.m. to 7:00 p.m.; Friday and Saturday: 9:00 a.m. to 5:00 p.m.
Rio Grande Valley Civil War Trail Mobile Web: 956–847–3002; **Extension:** 2207

Jackson Ranch

Along the Rio Grande in Hidalgo County lies the Jackson Ranch and Eli Jackson Cemetery, once owned by Nathaniel Jackson, a Unionist during the Civil War. In the 1850s, Jackson left Alabama with his African American wife Matilda Hicks, his son Eli, and other adult children. They hoped to escape the intolerance of interracial marriage they had known in the South. Accompanying the Jacksons were eleven African American freedmen. In 1857, Jackson

Figure 3.6. Jackson Ranch Church, built in 1874.

founded his ranch on a former Spanish grant. There he operated a ferry on the Rio Grande. His property is said to have become a refuge for runaway slaves from Texas and the Deep South. Today, many people know about the Underground Railroad that shepherded enslaved people to freedom in the northern United States and Canada, but few know about the route to freedom in Mexico. The Jackson Ranch lay near the Military Highway between Fort Ringgold and Fort Brown, and was visited by Confederate and Union troops as they fought for control of the Lower Valley in 1863 and 1864. Jackson died in 1865, the same year that his son Eli established the family cemetery where members of the clan now rest. Nathaniel Jackson's grave is unmarked.

TEXAS HISTORICAL COMMISSION—HISTORICAL MARKER #2706
JACKSON RANCH CHURCH
This fellowship was founded in 1874 by the Rev. Alexander H. Sutherland (1848–1911), an early Methodist missionary, on Juan Manuel de La Vina's El Capote Ranch. In 1883 the congregation began meeting near this site on the Jackson Ranch when owner Martin Jackson donated the land. He later built a small chapel for their use. In 1910 most of the church members moved to the new city of McAllen, and only a few families continued to worship here. As

92   Chapter 3

one of the first Protestant congregations in Hidalgo County, this church has continued to serve area residents. (1983)

TEXAS HISTORICAL COMMISSION—HISTORICAL MARKER #13730
ELI JACKSON CEMETERY
In 1857, Nathaniel Jackson came from Alabama and established a ranch in this area. A former slave owner, Jackson, who was white, came with his wife Matilda Hicks, who was black, their children and his freed slaves. On his 5,500-acre ranch, Jackson raised livestock and grew vegetables, cotton and sugarcane. He also established a chapel that served family and friends. He was known for his generosity and hospitality, and many, including runaway slaves, came to the ranch in need of lodging and other resources. Upon Jackson's death in 1865, his heirs divided the property. The share to his son Eli included this site, the family cemetery. Eli and his wife, Elizabeth Kerr, and their children continued the family tradition of hospitality. Eli served a county official, as did his son Nathaniel "Polo" Jackson. Polo's daughter Adela operated the ranch and cared for the cemetery until her death in 1992. Today, the Eli Jackson Cemetery represents the early area ranching communities. The burial ground is a tie to the Jackson family, and to their friends and neighbors from the past who share this as a final resting place. Historic Texas Cemetery–2005

Location: (From Cemeteries of Texas): Drive south of Pharr on US 281 to Fay's Corners, where Highway 281 turns east. Stay on 281 and go east 0.8 mile; then turn south and cross the canal levee; go 0.4 mile, turn east toward the church spire, about 0.2 mile. The cemetery is 500 feet northeast of the church, against the canal embankment.
GPS Coordinates: Latitude 26° 05' 08.35" N Longitude 98° 11' 03.83" W
Access: No known restrictions at this time.
Rio Grande Valley Civil War Trail Mobile Web: 956-847-3002; **Extension:** 2205

Webber's Ranch

Located not far from the Jackson Ranch was the property of their neighbor John Webber. Webber's Ranch and cemetery lies beside the Rio Grande near the old Military Highway, south of Donna in Hidalgo County. John Ferdinand Webber, a Vermont native, was among the earliest Anglo-American settlers in Texas. In 1832, he resided in Wells Prairie, south of Austin, which eventually developed into the village of Webberville. There he bought the freedom of Silvia Hector, an enslaved African-American woman. He married Silvia and adopted her children. As more settlers from the Deep South moved into the area, discrimination grew against Webber and his family. In 1853, the Webbers moved to the border with its more tolerant racial attitude. Here Juan Fernando Webber, as he was known locally, bought acreage from Spanish land grants and established his rancho. During the Civil War, Webber and his growing family remained loyal to the Union. For his own safety, Webber crossed into Mexico while Confederate troops occupied the Valley. In June, 1864, Confederate forces led by John S. Ford and Santos Benavides drove the Union troops back toward Brownsville. At the ranch, the Confederates arrested Webber's sons as Union sympathizers, but one son escaped, rode to Brownsville, and told the Union commander that Ford had only sixty men. Union troops were dispatched to find the enemy but Ford struck first, scattering the Union force. John Webber returned to his ranch after the war ended and died there in 1882. His wife, nicknamed "Aunt Puss," survived him by nine years. Both lie in the ranch cemetery, along with other family members and ranch workers.

Location: Donna, TX, in Hidalgo County. Drive south from Donna on State 493 to US 281, the Military Highway; turn west and go 2.8 miles, and then

Figure 3.7. Webber Ranch Cemetery, with John Ferdinand Webber's military headstone.

turn south on the road (unimproved) to the Donna Pumping Station. The cemetery is approximately 260 yards east, next to the levee.
GPS Coordinates: Latitude 26° 04′ 17.65″ N Longitude 98° 06′ 10.45″ W
Access: Access to the cemetery is restricted.
Rio Grande Valley Civil War Trail Mobile Web: 956-847-3002; **Extension:** 2210

Relámpago Ranch

In 1852 Thaddeus Rhodes, county clerk, commissioner, and judge of the recently founded Hidalgo County, purchased land here. Four years later, José María Mora, a local rancher, purchased the adjoining property and with Rhodes established the Relámpago Ranch as co-owners. By 1860 they built a ranch house and port of entry half a mile north of the river. There Rhodes served as deputy tax collector and inspector. Later a small community and stagecoach stop developed.

TEXAS HISTORICAL COMMISSION—HISTORICAL MARKER# 4239
RELAMPAGO RANCH
Originally part of a Spanish land grant, Relámpago (lightning) Ranch community lay along the stage and military route from Rio Grande City to Brownsville. In 1852 Thaddeus Rhodes (1828–1904) acquired acreage here when he came as Hidalgo county clerk. Later he served as commissioner and judge. He and

Figure 3.8. Thaddeus Rhodes and family on Relámpago Ranch. Courtesy of University of Texas Rio Grande Valley Special Collection Archives.

Jose Maria Mora (1824–1884), who bought adjoining land about 1856, helped bring economic and social stability. Mora and later his son Melchior, a deputy sheriff and Texas Ranger, farmed, ranched, and had the only general store in the area. Descendants still live on the property. (1980)

Location: On US 281 west of FM 491
Rio Grande Valley Civil War Trail Mobile Web: 956–847–3002; **Extension:** 2211

Battle of La Bolsa Bend

Now dry, La Bolsa, or "the pocket," was a meander of the Rio Grande on the boundary between Hidalgo and Cameron counties. On February 4, 1860, Mexican rancher, politician, military leader, outlaw, and folk hero Juan Cortina attacked the silver-laden steamboat *Ranchero* as it navigated La Bolsa en route to Brownsville. This was one major event in what is sometimes referred to as the "Cortina War," an armed conflict between various local elite groups that became enmeshed with the Civil War when it reached the Valley in 1861.

Figure 3.9. Google Earth image to show the location of the Battle at La Bolsa Bend (the pocket), formerly located at a bend in the Rio Grande, now shows as a dried resaca to the north of the contemporary flow of the river.

Soldiers from Fort Ringgold were onboard the steamboat to guard the valuable cargo. Texas Rangers from Rio Grande City rode along the north bank as added security; more Rangers and a US Cavalry troop from Fort Brown also approached from the east. All of these forces converged on La Bolsa.

As the *Ranchero* entered the narrow bend, the Cortinistas opened fire from the south bank. Those on board returned fire with rifles and two cannons. As Cortina prepared a second attack, Col. John S. "Rip" Ford and Texas Rangers from Rio Grande City crossed the river on the *Ranchero* and charged Cortina's position. The Cortinistas and their leader retreated, leaving behind many dead.

The *Ranchero* delivered her cargo safely to Fort Brown, but in the wake of the incident, the US Army sent Lt. Col. Robert E. Lee from San Antonio to the Rio Grande with orders to inform the Mexican authorities that if they could not corral Cortina, the US Army would enter Mexico in order to do so. For a time, Juan Cortina withdrew south, into the Mexican interior, but he returned to the border in 1861 as a Union officer to resume his war with local rivals, particularly Confederate commander Santos Benavides.

TEXAS HISTORICAL COMMISSION—HISTORICAL MARKER #323
BATTLE OF LA BOLSA
In 1859 and early 1860 a series of raids on Texas settlements led by Juan N. Cortina (1824–1894) led to skirmishes with companies of Texas Rangers and U.S. soldiers. These conflicts became known as the Cortina War. On February 4, 1860, a battle occurred at La Bolsa Bend (ca. 1 mi. S.) between Cortina's raiders and Captain John S. "Rip" Ford's Texas Rangers. The Rangers successfully defended the riverboat "Ranchero," traveling downstream from Rio Grande City, from an attack by Cortina's band. Cortina escaped into Mexico and later became a general in the Mexican Army.

Location: Located on boundary line between Hidalgo and Cameron counties. Texas state historical marker is located on US 281 (Military Highway), 4 miles east of Progresso, Texas.
GPS Coordinates: Latitude 26° 05′ 04.84″ N Longitude 97° 52′ 11.47″ W
Access: Original river bed where the battle occurred is now dry land. It may be viewed in part from the marker site. Current border security conditions may impede or prohibit direct access.
Contact: Contact local office of the US Border Patrol (McAllen, Texas) for

information about site access and security. US Customs and Border Patrol Office, McAllen: 956-217-3700. Access to the historical marker is unrestricted.

Rio Grande Valley Civil War Trail Mobile Web: 956-847-3002; Extension: 2202

Veteran's War Memorial of Texas—All Wars Memorial

This expansive park, located at the McAllen Convention Center complex, is designed to provide visitors with an educational, cultural, and historical experience. It serves to teach and inspire future generations about the sacrifices of those who died in the service of their country. Every year, the city of McAllen sponsors memorial services here on Veteran's Day, Memorial Day, and Pearl Harbor Day.

The Texas Daughters of the American Revolution (TXDAR) Plaza of Liberty was started by Texas State Regent Pamela Wright, who erected the first three memorial walls and the statue of Patrick Henry. Current state regent, Judy Ostler, added three additional walls and a statue of George Washington. The portion of the plaza that memorializes the American Revolution through the US Civil War era was dedicated on April 18, 2015. One of the engraved

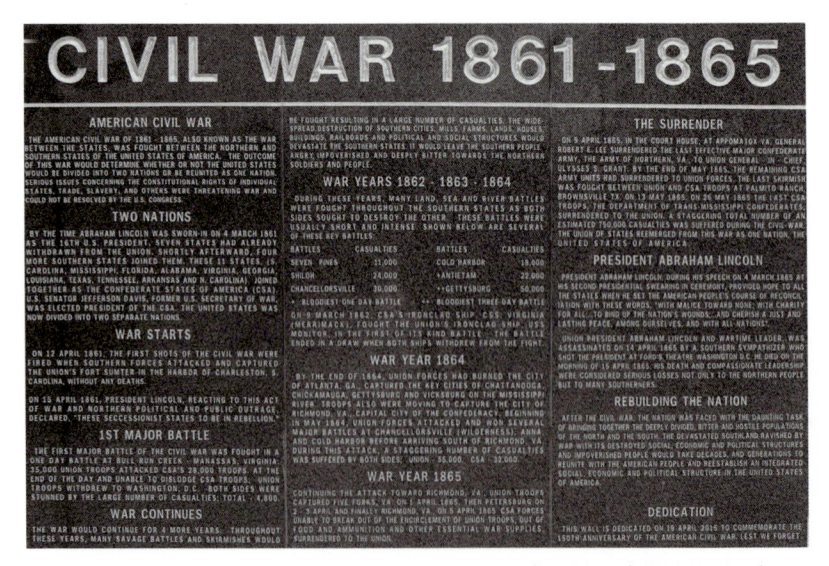

Figure 3.10. Dedicated Civil War engraved granite stone panel at Veteran's War Memorial Park, McAllen, Texas.

Figure 3.11. Obelisk at War Veterans Memorial Park, McAllen, Texas.

granite panels focuses on the last land battle of the Civil War at Palmito Ranch, while others discuss the larger conflict including Bull Run, Shiloh, Antietam, Vicksburg, and Gettysburg. On April 19, 2016, the Rio Grande Chapter of the DAR added three bronze bas-relief panels commemorating World War I with funding from a grant by the National DAR.

Also at the site is a Medal of Honor Plaza that includes the names of all Medal of Honor recipients from the state of Texas, including soldiers who served during the Civil War.

The Veterans War Memorial of Texas is developing educational resources that include lesson plans and supporting materials that are aligned with the requirements of the Texas Essential Knowledge and Skills (TEKS) established by the Texas Education Administration (TEA).

Location: 3129 Galveston Avenue, McAllen, TX 78501, adjacent to the McAllen Convention Center and the McAllen Performing Arts Center at Expressway 83 (Interstate 2) and Ware Roads

GPS Coordinates: Latitude 26° 11′ 56.93″ N Longitude 98° 15′ 21.98″ W

Access: Park is open at all times.

Contact: Col. Frank Plummer, 956–631–2511, plummerf@att.net

Further Reading

Amberson, Mary, James A McAllen, and Margaret H McAllen. *I Would Rather Sleep in Texas: A History of the Lower Rio Grande Valley and the People of the Santa Anita Land Grant.* College Station: Texas State Historical Assn Press, 2014.

Stambaugh, J. Lee and Lillian J. Stambaugh, *The Lower Rio Grande Valley of Texas*, San Antonio: The Naylor Company, 1954.

STARR
COUNTY
RIO
GRANDE
CITY
Old City Cemetery
Mifflin Kenedy
Warehouse
Fort Ringgold
Robert E. Lee House
755
83
ROMA
649
RIO
GRANDE
CITY

4

Starr County Sites and Events

Starr County lies at the midpoint of the two hundred mile long Rio Grande Valley Civil War Trail. Roma and Rio Grande City are the largest municipalities in the county. Both played significant roles during the American Civil War. These two communities formed around earlier Spanish colonial ranching villages associated with Nuevo Santander, the province founded by José de Escandón in the middle of the eighteenth century. They are respectively located across the Rio Grande or Rio Bravo from Mier, Ciudad Miguel Aleman, and Camargo. The Rio Grande was instrumental to the prosperity of these towns as a thoroughfare for commerce and trade.

The villages of Camargo and Mier were settled in 1749 and 1753, respectively. Blas María de la Garza Falcón was the captain and chief justice of the Camargo settlement, and Jose Florencio de Chapa was captain of the Mier settlement. In 1752, Garza Falcón established a ranch on the north side of the river called Rancho Carnestolenda (referring to the three-day carnival period before lent during which one can still eat meat). A decade later in the mid-1760s, the Saenz brothers (Miguel and Santiago) established a ranch known as Corrales de Saenz, fifteen miles downstream from Mier. This ranch evolved into a larger community known as Roma-Los Saenz, which included a settlement called San Pedro de Roma on the southern (Mexican) bank of the river. Today, Camargo is the sister city to Rio Grande City and San Pedro de Roma, which today is known as Miguel Alemán, is linked to Roma.

In addition to their access to river traffic, both town sites stand on a land

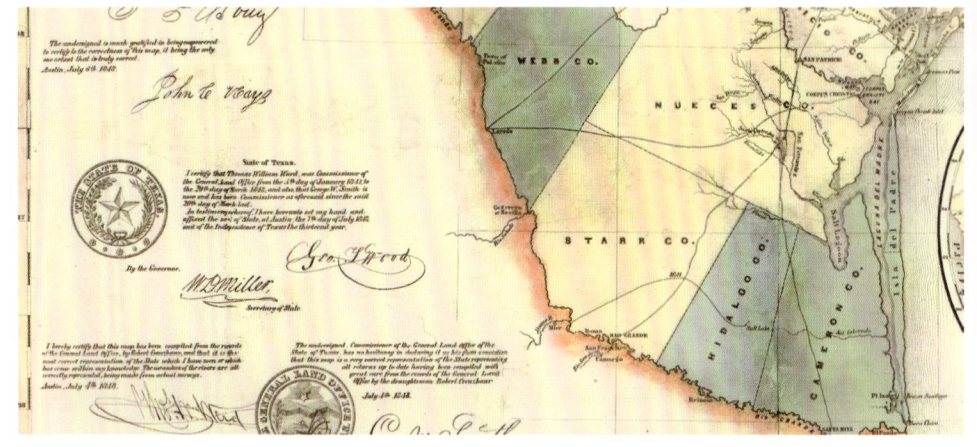

Figure 4.1. Texas General Land Office map of the State of Texas by J. De Cordova in 1854. Note pathways forged by Native American peoples that cross the Rio Grande specifically at the Rio Alamo (near Mier/Roma) and the Rio San Juan (near Camargo/Rio Grande City). These pathways eventually lead to the salt lakes found in today's Hidalgo County. Courtesy of the Texas General Land Office (map #93903).

path known as the Paseo de los Indios, which led to the salt lakes located in northern Hidalgo County. Salt, a mineral used to cure and preserve meat among other things, had been mined at the salt lakes for centuries, and perhaps for millennia by Native Americans in the region.

Almost a century after the establishment of Rancho Carnestolendas, Henry Clay Davis arrived in Camargo. In early 1846, shortly after arriving, Davis married María Hilaria de la Garza, owner of the lands on which Rio Grande City now stands. Three months later, with the outbreak of the Mexican-American War, Davis became a volunteer with the American forces. His ranch then became known as Rancho Davis or Davis Ranch. During the war, steamboats plied the waters of the Rio Grande, transporting troops and supplies. It was at this time that Davis Ranch became known as Davis Landing, a busy inland port on the river. Throughout the conflict, Davis hosted Zachary Taylor's troops. Following the conflict, the US Army purchased 150 acres of land adjacent to Davis Landing and on October 26, 1848, established Camp Ringgold. The camp was located one hundred miles from both Fort Brown in Brownsville and Fort McIntosh in Laredo. With the founding of Ringgold, other discharged soldiers decided to stay in Rio Grande City, as they saw the potential to profit economically through commerce with the adjacent military base and the

Mexican port town across the river. Camp Ringgold became known as Ringgold Barracks during the Civil War era.

Starr County was established in 1848 and was named after James Harper Starr, Texas' first president of the board of land commissioners. Henry Clay Davis, together with Capt. Forbes Britton, surveyed and platted Rio Grande City as the Starr County seat. The first Starr county courthouse, which is the oldest original courthouse still standing in the state of Texas, is today known as the Mifflin Kenedy Warehouse on Water Street.

Rio Grande City and Roma are thirteen-and-a-half miles apart. Visitors traveling the Rio Grande Valley Civil War Trail can see all the sites in Starr County within one day. Each town has a tourism center. The Kelsey-Bass Museum and Event Center in Rio Grande City, located at 101 South Washington Street (956- 487–0672), serves as a visitor's center and the city hall. Also, visitors may explore Rio Grande City's backstreets, hidden places, and points of interest by trolley on the Bessie III (a fee is charged). Tours operate Monday through Friday from 10:00 a.m. to 1:30 p.m. (For reservations, call 956–488–0047 or visit their website at www.rgcedc.org.) For those interested in natural history and native wildlife, Rancho Lomitas, located eight miles north of Rio Grande City, is a must. (For tour information, call 956–486–2576 or email info@rancholomitas.com.)

Rio Grande City

The historic plaza on Britton Avenue in Rio Grande City is anchored on the north end by the current Starr County courthouse and on the south end by a gazebo with two historical markers. Formerly located at the corner of Britton and Mirasoles Streets was the home of Henry Clay Davis and María Hilaria de la Garza. Demolished in 1995, this sandstone structure was originally built

Figure 4.2. Historic plaza in Rio Grande City, as seen in the early 1900s. Courtesy of the Rio Grande City Independent School District.

as a two-story home. During the Civil War era, the banks of the Rio Grande were just beyond Water Street, the southern border of the courthouse plaza. The steamboat landing was located where Britton Street met the river. Britton Street was named after Capt. Forbes Britton, who surveyed the plat for the town site. Britton was known to partner in business ventures with other prominent regional entrepreneurs such as Charles Stillman of Cameron County and John Redmond of Zapata County.

TEXAS HISTORICAL COMMISSION MARKER—CIVIL WAR MEMORIAL #4270 RIO GRANDE CITY, C.S.A.
An official Confederate port of entry, customhouse and major terminus of the cotton road to Mexico. Cotton was the one great money crop of the South that could be sold to hungry European mills for cash for necessary arms, munitions, drugs that had to come from Europe. International ports on the Rio Grande were the South's frail lifelines, its last resource in a war with an industrialized North that manufactured for its self what the South had to import. Cotton arrived at this booming border town on wagons and oxcarts after a hot and dusty trip. It was then ferried across the river and delivered to the neutral ships anchored in the Gulf. Teamsters loaded vital leather goods, clothing, blankets, guns, ammunition and medical supplies for the return trip. Troops from nearby Fort Ringgold guarded the wagon trains and town from bandit raids. In November 1863 Federal forces captured Brownsville and the 1st Texas Union Cavalry advanced up river, captured and occupied this town, seizing the cotton awaiting entry. Rio Grande City was reoccupied in May 1864 and used as a supply and reserve base for the recapture of Brownsville. There was constant danger here from raids by Mexican guerrillas paid by enemy agents to make trouble in Texas. Draft evaders, Union sympathizers and those wanting to avoid conflicts of war tried to cross the river here. In an arrangement with Mexican officials, Confederates both required and checked passports to curb desertions and smuggling.

LOS CAMINOS DEL RIO MARKER— HISTORIC RIO GRANDE CITY
Perhaps one of the oldest settlements in South Texas, Rio Grande City is located on lands once settled by Spanish colonizer José de Escandón in 1749. The site was part of a ranching community known as "Rancho Carnestolendas" established in 1753 by Don José Antonio de la Garza Falcón [son of Blas María

de la Garza Falcón]. During the 1830s the ranch was under the ownership of Don Francisco de la Garza Martinez, a direct descendant of Garza Falcón.

In 1846 Henry Clay Davis a Kentuckian who came to the area as a volunteer with the Texas forces married María Hilaria de la Garza the daughter of Francisco de la Garza Martinez. As a precondition of that marriage Davis was instructed to settle on the north side of the river to oversee operations of the ranch. Two years later, Davis designed the town as a river port with broad streets modeled after the capital city of Austin, Texas.

In 1848 Fort Ringgold was established and assured the town's growth and permanence and in 1849 the town received their first post office. During the 19th century, Rio Grande City had an active passenger and cargo ship trade with New Orleans and flourished as a cattle center.

As border disputes and racial tensions arose in the area they helped give rise to several incidents, one of which was the Juan Cortina Battle of 1859 in Rio Grande City, the Rio Grande City riot of 1888 in which the Mexican population was pitted against the Anglo controlled sheriff's office, and yet another incident members of the black Ninth United States Cavalry fired toward the town in 1899 amid reports of a civilian attack on the garrison.

Juan Cortina Battle

Born in 1824 to an aristocratic family with a large land grant in South Texas, Juan Cortina saw his property and those of his neighbors threatened by the US acquisition of Texas. Cortina recruited an armed force that fought on both sides of the new border. In what became known as the First Cortina War, he and his army took control of Brownsville. Following negotiations with Mexican authorities, Cortina retreated but issued a proclamation asserting the rights of Mexicans and Tejanos, and demanded punishment of anyone who violated those rights. Tensions arose between Cortina and the Texas Rangers. In December 1859, the Rangers, led by John S. "Rip" Ford and Maj. Samuel P. Heintzelman, pursued Cortina's army. In a battle in Rio Grande City, Cortina was defeated, losing sixty men. He and his surviving followers retreated into Mexico after attempting to capture the steamboat *Ranchero*, owned by Cortina's hated enemies Mifflin Kenedy and Richard King. With the outbreak of the US Civil War in May 1861, Cortina's army invaded the town of Zapata and was defeated by Confederate officer Col. Santos Benavides. Regarded by Anglos as an outlaw, he is remembered by many in the Valley as a heroic figure who fought for the rights of Hispanic people. Cortina became involved in Mexico's own civil war against the French, later serving as governor of Tamaulipas and commander of the Mexican Army of the North. He died in Mexico, exiled from his family's land grant, in 1894 (see fig. 1.5).

Located near the south end of Rio Grande City's central plaza is the marker for the Cortina Battle, at the point where Britton Street meets East Main Street (Highway 83). The Juan Cortina Battle occurred on December 27, 1859. This conflict sparked Robert E. Lee's visit to Fort Ringgold in 1860, where he had to deal with the "Cortina matter."

> **TEXAS HISTORICAL COMMISSION—MARKER #4762**
> **SITE OF CORTINA BATTLE, DEC. 27, 1859**
> Crushing defeat for partisan leader Juan Cortina who late in 1859 laid waste to the Lower Rio Grande Valley. Cortina's band of 450 were surprised here at daybreak by Major S. P. Heintzleman with U. S. Army troops, joined by Texas Rangers recruited by John S. ("RIP") Ford. Cortina fled to Mexico by horseback. Many of his men jumped into the Rio Grande. Regarrisoning of Ringgold Barracks put an end to partisan raids for a time. But with the American Civil War (1861–1865) and Cortina's rise to power in Tamaulipas, raids were renewed until Cortina was removed in 1875.

Location: 100 East Main Street, Rio Grande City, TX 78582 (south side of street, east of Britton Street)
GPS Coordinates: Latitude 26° 22' 44.36" N Longitude 98° 49' 14.27" W
Access: Marked with a Texas Historical Commission Marker—open access
Rio Grande Valley Civil War Trail Mobile Web: 956–847–3002; **Extension:** 2402

Ringgold Barracks

Atop a river bluff from which two nations are visible, army engineers in 1848 established Camp Ringgold. After the Mexican-American War, the Mexican government was forced to give up its claims to territory in Texas and the Southwest. Acting upon Mexican requests, the US Army built forts along the Rio Grande from Brownsville to Eagle Pass, placing them 100 miles apart. Camp Ringgold, later Ringgold Barracks, was named for Maj. Samuel Ringgold, who was killed at the battle of Palo Alto in 1846. Nearby stood the settlement of

Rancho Davis, later renamed Rio Grande City. During the Civil War, Ringgold changed hands several times, starting in 1861 when it was occupied by Confederate forces. Late in 1863, Union troops re-entered the Rio Grande Valley and seized the camp, only for it to be seized again by rebels led by Cols. John S. "Rip" Ford and Santos Benavides. Because of their efforts, the post stayed in Confederate hands until the end of the war. After 1865, the post was renamed Fort Ringgold and was updated with permanent brick buildings. African American troops, including US Colored Troops and later segregated African American US regulars (the "Buffalo Soldiers"), were quartered here until the early twentieth century, protecting the region from border unrest. Black soldiers at Ringgold endured prejudice and discrimination that led to an outbreak of racial violence in 1899. Following a similar incident in Brownsville in 1906, the African American units were permanently withdrawn from the region. In 1944, during World War II, Fort Ringgold was closed and the 124th Cavalry was sent to the Southeast Asian theatre of the war.

It has been stated that Fort Ringgold is the best preserved nineteenth century US Army post in the United States. There, dozens of buildings constructed after 1850 and into the beginning of the twentieth century may be seen. The only pre–Civil War era structure is the (wooden) Robert E. Lee House. A nonprofit organization, "Revive Fort Ringgold" is undertaking the task of restoring

Figure 4.3. Wooden structures of Ringgold Barracks, Fort Ringgold. Courtesy of the Rio Grande City Independent School District.

Figure 4.4. Confederate Colonel John Salmon "Rip" Ford. Courtesy of the DeGolyer Library, Southern Methodist University.

the site and is currently in the process of placing wayside markers throughout the grounds on the historic buildings.

In 1967, twenty-three years after Fort Ringgold was decommissioned, the US Army returned to the site following the September landfall of Hurricane Beulah. The former fort was then serving as the home of the Rio Grande City Independent School District. During the flooding associated with the storm, the US Army evacuated stranded families, numbering nearly 14,000 people, from both the Mexican and American sides of the river to shelter and receive medical attention at the old fort. A few weeks later at the beginning of October 1967, the evacuees returned to their homes north and south of the Rio Grande and the US Army, once again, vacated the fort.

TEXAS HISTORICAL COMMISSION—MARKER #2012
FORT RINGGOLD
Established October 26, 1848, at Davis Landing by Capt. J. H. La Motte, 1st U. S. Infantry, as Ringgold Barracks. Named in honor of Brevet Major David Ringgold, 4th U. S. Artillery, who died of wounds received at Palo Alto, May 8, 1846. Troops were withdrawn March 3, 1859. Reoccupied December 29, 1859. Abandoned in 1861. Reoccupied by U. S. troops in June 1865. General Robert E. Lee passed a few days here in 1856 and in 1860.

Figure 4.5. Hospital building at Fort Ringgold. Courtesy of the Rio Grande City Independent School District.

Figure 4.6. Hospital building at Fort Ringgold, contemporary view.

Figure 4.7. Enlisted men's barracks at Fort Ringgold. Courtesy of the Rio Grande City Independent School District.

Figure 4.8. Enlisted men's barracks at Fort Ringgold, contemporary view.

Figure 4.9 Officer's Row at Fort Ringgold. Courtesy of the Rio Grande City Independent School District.

Figure 4.10. Rear view of officer's quarters at Fort Ringgold with stables to the left, contemporary view. These are two-story duplexes. The one-story extension in the rear housed a kitchen and a stable where each cavalry officer maintained his own horse. According to local folklore, there is a ghost that resides on the second floor of one of these buildings.

113

Figure 4.11. Stables at Fort Ringgold, contemporary view.

Figure 4.12 Morgue building at Fort Ringgold, contemporary view.

TEXAS HISTORICAL COMMISSION—MARKER #2013
FORT RINGGOLD C.S.A.
Occupied early in Civil War by Texas Confederates under Col. John S. Ford. Vital in chain of posts used to defend the 2,000 mile Texas frontier, coastline and border always threatened by attacks from Indians, bandits and Federal troops. Cols. Ford, August Buchel and Santos Benavides had troops here from time to time to scout the river, defend ranches and guard wagons trading cotton for war supplies in neutral Mexico. Taken in November 1863 by 1st Texas Union Cavalry. Retaken May 1864 by Ford and used as base to recapture Brownsville.

Location: Ringgold Barracks/Fort Ringgold, Rio Grande City, TX 78582
GPS Coordinates: Latitude 26° 22′ 27.67″ N Longitude 98° 48′ 30.45″ W
Access: (Hours of operation) Visitors are permitted to drive or walk throughout the campus in order to view the buildings that survive today. There is no access to any of the buildings, except for the Robert E. Lee House (by appointment; see next entry).
Contact: 956-488-0047
Rio Grande Valley Civil War Trail Mobile Web: 956-847-3002; **Extension:** 2408
Interesting Facts: In 1909 the Fort Ringgold Post Cemetery was closed and the bodies reburied at Alexandria National Cemetery in Pineville, Louisiana. Visitors there will find a granite memorial dated 1911 to the sixteen unknown federal soldiers who were reinterred at Alexandria National Cemetery. In December of 2014, Revive Fort Ringgold was formed, a 501c3 organization seeking private donations and public entities to help refurbish, rebuild, and preserve Fort Ringgold. Donations will be used to establish a fort museum, conduct tours, and promote and enrich the local economy by establishing the fort as a tourist destination and promoting an interest in local history. Contact them at 956-716-6700, www.fortringgoldtx.org, or fortringgoldtx@gmail.com.

Robert E. Lee House
At the heart of historic Fort Ringgold stands the original Commandant's Quarters. The house dates to the 1850s. During the Civil War, the house saw Union and Confederate troops alternately abandon and then reoccupy the

post. From its south-facing front porch, soldiers watched steamboats coming up the Rio Grande, and surveyed the distant Mexican landscape beyond it. Today, low trees mark the original bluff along the river, which shifted away many years ago.

Figure 4.13. Robert E. Lee House at Fort Ringgold in 1860. Courtesy of the Rio Grande City Independent School District.

Figure 4.14. Robert E. Lee House after renovations at Fort Ringgold.

One famous guest was Lt. Col. Robert E. Lee, later a Confederate general. He visited Ringgold Barracks in 1856 for court-martial duty, and again in 1860, while dealing with the aftermath of Juan Cortina's raid at La Bolsa Bend. In the field, Lee usually preferred to sleep in his tent; however, as a guest of the post commandant, he may have shared quarters in this house, giving rise to its popular name, the "Robert E. Lee House." The house is currently occupied by the Robert E. Lee House Museum.

Location: Robert E. Lee House/Commandants Quarters at Fort Ringgold, 1 South Ringgold Street, Rio Grande City, TX 78582
GPS Coordinates: Latitude 26° 22′ 26.19″ N Longitude 98° 48′ 32.10″ W
Access: Contact City Tourism to schedule your visit.
Contact: 956-488-0047
Rio Grande Valley Civil War Trail Mobile Web: 956-847-3002; **Extension:** 2409

Mifflin Kenedy Warehouse

In 1850, Richard King, Mifflin Kenedy, and two others formed a steamboat company to carry cargo on the Rio Grande. The company achieved almost total control of the shipping along the Rio Grande during the 1850s, until 1874 when the company was dissolved. The Mifflin Kenedy Warehouse, where the company stored cotton and other goods, is the last reminder of this era, which included the Civil War.

Figure 4.15. Mifflin Kenedy Warehouse at the corner of Water and Texas Streets in Rio Grande City, Texas. This building served as the first courthouse in Starr County.

The Mifflin Kenedy warehouse was built in 1854, near the steamboat landing on Water Street, Rio Grande City. It would serve as the first county courthouse and later became an official Confederate port of entry, customhouse, and major terminus of the cotton route to Mexico. The cotton bales would arrive by the wagon load at river ports such as Rio Grande City. There they were warehoused, and then ferried down the Rio Grande to the Mexican port of Bagdad and thence transported to neutral ships in the Gulf of Mexico. The ships would bring back leather, clothing, blankets, guns, ammunition, and medical supplies. In 1864 the 1st US Texas Cavalry captured Ringgold Barracks from its Confederate occupiers and seized the cotton that was stored in this warehouse.

Location: 203 West Water Street, Rio Grande City, TX 78582 (at Texas Street)
GPS Coordinates: Latitude 26° 22′ 41.84″ N Longitude 98° 49′ 16.11″ W
Access: Occupied by the City of Rio Grande City Public Works Office. Not open to the public.
Rio Grande Valley Civil War Trail Mobile Web: 956–847–3002;
Extension: 2404

Old Rio Grande City Cemetery

In the same year that the territory north of the Rio Grande was grafted onto the United States by the Treaty of Guadalupe Hidalgo, Rio Grande City residents Henry Clay Davis and María Hilaria Davis donated land for a city cemetery. Burials at the site began soon afterward. Davis (1814–66), a Mexican War veteran, and his wife, María Hilaria de la Garza-Davis, are buried in the center of the cemetery. The cemetery is the location of the graves of multiple Civil War veterans as well, such as Union Army Quartermaster Lino Hinojosa and local merchant and Union sympathizer Peter John Kelsey.

When making the trip from Rio Grande City to Roma, be sure to stop at the Los Saenz Cemetery on the eastern approach to Roma to see the *monjonera*. A mojonera is a large, pointed stone that marks the original boundary for a *porción* (land grant portion). The cemetery is on the eastbound side of US Highway 83 and the engraved stone marker, which marks porción number 74, is protected by an iron barrier and is within the cemetery grounds, very close to the street. It is engraved with the number of the land grant, the year, and

Figure 4.16. Sergeant Lino Hinojosa and his brother-in-law Sgt. Luis Gonzales. Hinojosa served in the Union Army as quartermaster sergeant in the 2nd Texas Cavalry and is buried in Rio Grande City's Old City Cemetery. Courtesy of Eva Hinojosa.

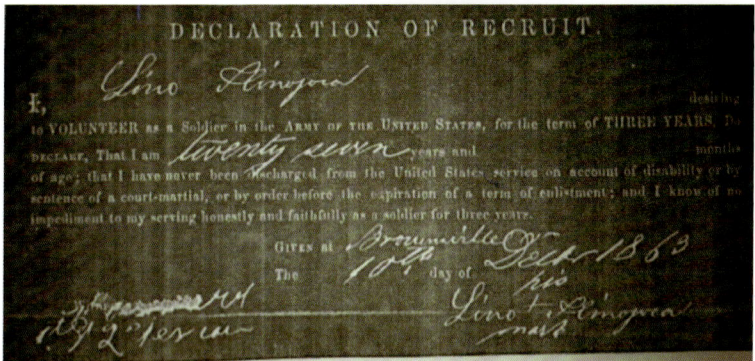

Figure 4.17. Signed declaration of volunteer service into the Union Army at Brownsville, Texas, by Lino Hinojosa on December 10, 1863. Courtesy of the University of Texas Rio Grande Valley Special Collections Library and Archives.

initials of the surveyor, and is one of the few existing stone mojoneras in its original location.

Thirteen miles west of Rio Grande City is the Roma Historic District, which contains the current City Hall building. There at the intersection of Lincoln and North Water Streets, you will find the Roma Bluffs World Birding Center. It is open seasonally during the months of October through March, Wednesday

Starr County Sites and Events

Figure 4.18. Original *mojonera*, or cornerstone, of *porción* 74 at Los Saenz Cemetery in Starr County. This pointed stone is etched with the surveyor's initials, the year, and the porcion number, and was used to mark the boundary between Spanish land grants during the mid-1700s.

through Saturday, from 8:00 a.m. to 5:00 p.m., However, special tours can be arranged by calling City Hall (956- 849–1411). The observation deck on the river bluff provides an uninterrupted view of the Rio Grande and the Mexican city of Miguel Alemán.

Location: Old Rio Grande City Cemetery, 500 West 2nd Street, Rio Grande City, TX 78582 (It takes up the entire block of 2nd Street and Main Street/US Highway 83.)

GPS Coordinates: Latitude 26° 22' 50.82" N Longitude 98° 49' 27.30" W

Access: Open access

Rio Grande Valley Civil War Trail Mobile Web: 956–847–3002; **Extension:** 2405

Roma Historic District

Situated at the farthest inland point for steamboat navigation on the Rio Grande, the city of Roma became a major center in the movement of cotton from the interior of Texas during the Civil War. Bales of cotton were transferred from wagons to boats in the town center and then shipped down the officially neutral river to the Mexican port of Bagdad, where it was legally exported

Figure 4.19. World Birding Visitor's Center at Roma Bluffs on the historic plaza in Roma, Texas.

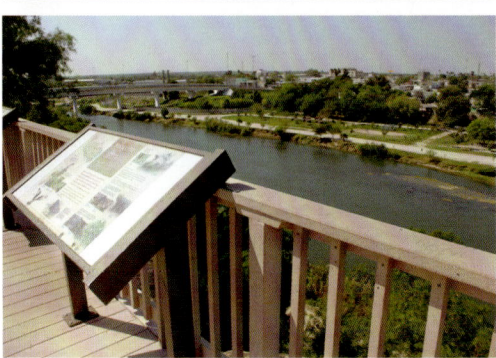

Figure 4.20. Front view of World Birding Center Observation Deck at Roma Bluffs, with rear view toward Mexico.

to manufacturers in Europe. This trade was crucial in financing the Confederate war effort. After the war, Roma continued to be a river trading center until the 1880s, when lowered river levels prevented commercial navigation and the city fell into obscurity. Because of this economic downturn, however, much of the historic architecture has been preserved, including numerous sites that were important during the Civil War era. One such structure is the Rodriguez House in the Wharf Area at the corner of Juárez and Portscheller Streets. During the Civil War, this building served as a warehouse for the cotton traffic moving down the river. Nearby, in the Plaza Area, is the Leocadia Garcia House, which was built by Swedish immigrant John Vale, the upper floor of which was a residence and the lower floor a mercantile business during the Civil War era. At the other end of the plaza is Our Lady of Refuge Roman Catholic Church, which was built during the mid-1850s and was the spiritual center for the town during the tumultuous period when Roma played such a key role in the Civil War struggle. The Roma Historic District was listed in the National Register of Historic Places in 1972 and was designated a National Historic Landmark in 1993.

Location: Roma Historic District, Convent Street between Estrella and North Water Streets, Roma, TX 78584

Figure 4.21. Historic Roma, Texas, United States and Mexican Boundary Survey, 1853.

Figure 4.22. Mid-twentieth century view of the historic Roma Plaza. Ramirez House and Memorial Hospital, built in 1853, on the right. Our Lady of Refuge Church in the center background.

GPS Coordinates: Latitude 26° 24' 22.36" N Longitude 98° 01' 03.54" W
Access: Tours arranged by appointment
Contact: Roma City Hall: 956-849-1411; Roma Historical Commission Chairman Noel Benavides: 956-844-9219
Rio Grande Valley Civil War Trail Mobile Web: 956-847-3002; **Extension:** 2407
Interesting Facts: The 1952 film *Viva Zapata!*, which starred Marlon Brando and Anthony Quinn, was filmed partially on Roma's plaza and in the Vale/Cox house.

John Vale

Along the Rio Grande, the years of the American Civil War were locally known as *Los Dias de Algodon*, or the "Cotton Times." These were prosperous times for riverside residents and entrepreneurs involved in the export of cotton to Mexico. One such person was John Vale. Vale brokered bales of cotton for the Confederacy and transported them across and down the river to Bagdad. Letters between José San Roman, a Spanish merchant in Matamoros, and John Vale, who operated out of Roma and its sister town across the river San Pedro de Roma (today Miguel Alemán), reveal much about the scale of the trade and conditions in the region. Vale informed San Roman that carts to transport cotton were in short supply, and that without payment his 286 bales of cotton would not pass the customs collector at Mier. Vale later reported that he had secured fifty carts at a rate of $5.00 per day. He also reported that he found

San Pedro to be a disagreeable place, where he had to hire watchmen for fear that the bales of cotton would be set on fire.

John Vale/Noah Cox House

The John Vale/Noah Cox House, located in Roma's Historic District, served as both a home and business location for John Heinrik Vale and Noah Cox, who were deeply embroiled in Civil War activities in Roma. Vale, a Swedish immigrant, had come to America in 1840 seeking adventure. During the Mexican-American War, Vale volunteered for Zachary Taylor's Army of Occupation and was encamped in Camargo. He chose to remain in the region, marrying a woman from Ciudad Mier in Tamaulipas and taking up residence across the Rio Grande in Roma. In 1853 he built a two-story home on the town's main plaza. Three years later, he sold the house to Cox, a representative of the New Orleans firm of Stadeker & Mecklinburger & Cox, who continued to use the house as both a residence and mercantile center. In addition to his mercantile operations during the Civil War, Cox also served in the Confederate Texas Cavalry. For his part, Vale engaged heavily in the lucrative cotton trade that funneled through the city of Roma during the Civil War, doing

Figure 4.23. John Henrik Vale, Confederate cotton trader and businessman in Roma, Texas, during the US Civil War (Swedish immigrant Johan Henrik Wallerius). Courtesy of the Vale family.

Figure 4.24. John Vale/Noah Cox House, located on the historic plaza in Roma, Texas. Both Vale and Cox were actively involved in Civil War—Vale as a cotton trader and Cox serving in the Confederate Texas Cavalry. Restoration of this structure by the City of Roma commenced in 2018.

business with Joseph Kleiber, a key player in Confederate business operations on the Gulf of Mexico.
Location: John Vale/Noah Cox House, Corner of Convent Avenue and North Water Street, Roma, TX 78584
GPS Coordinates: Latitude 26° 24′ 20.59″ N Longitude: 99° 01′ 08.35″ W
Access: House in ruins/not open to the public; on public historic district plaza
Rio Grande Valley Civil War Trail Mobile Web: 956–847–3002; **Extension:** 2403

Ramirez House/Ramirez Memorial Hospital

Two blocks from the steamboat landing site is this two-story stucco sandstone structure built in 1853 by Roma's first lawyer, Edward R. Hord. Born in Virginia, Hord arrived at the Rio Grande in 1846 with a volunteer regiment in the Mexican-American War. Through the 1860s, he served in the Texas State legislature and was a delegate to the Texas' secession meeting in 1861. During the American Civil War, Hord held the rank of colonel in John S. "Rip" Ford's cavalry. For a time, this building served as a military headquarters.

Figure 4.25. Contemporary view of the Ramirez House and Memorial Hospital building (right) on the Roma Historic Plaza. Our Lady of Refuge Church in the background.

Decades later the property was bought by Dr. Mario Ramirez, by whose name it is known today.

Location: Ramirez House/Ramirez Memorial Hospital, Corner of Convent Avenue and Estrella Street, Roma, TX 78584
GPS Coordinates: Latitude 26° 24' 22.06" N Longitude 99° 01' 03.37" W
Access: Not open to the public; on public historic district plaza
Rio Grande Valley Civil War Trail Mobile Web: 956–847–3002; **Extension:** 2406

Further Reading

Brooks Greene, Shirley. *When Rio Grande City Was Young*. Edinburg, TX: Pan American University, 1987.

Davis, L. Michael. *The Legendary Henry Clay Davis in Early Texas 1836–1866: Texas Ranger, Frontier Fighter, Enterprising Merchant, State Senator, Brigadier General and Founder of Rio Grande City*. Mission, TX: Author, February 2017.

Sanchez, Mario L., ed. *A Shared Experience: The History, Architecture, and Historic Designations of the Lower Rio Grande Heritage Corridor.* Austin: Los Caminos del Rio Heritage Project and the Texas Historical Commission, 1994.

Simmons, Thomas E. *Fort Ringgold: A Brief Tour.* Edinburg: University of Texas Pan American Press, 1991.

ZAPATA COUNTY

1. Confrontation at Carrizo
2. Confederate Reunion at La Soledad
3. Skirmish at Redmond's Ranch
4. The Reconstruction Era in Zapata

Zapata County Museum of History

ZAPATA

5

Zapata County Sites and Events

In 1858, a decade after the region's forcible annexation to Texas and the United States under the Treaty of Guadalupe Hidalgo, Zapata County was created from parts of Webb and Starr counties. Named in honor of Col. Antonio Zapata, a martyr of the short-lived (1840) Republic of the Rio Grande, the county seat was placed in Habitación, which was shortly thereafter renamed

Figure 5.1. Zapata County Museum of History houses bilingual exhibits depicting the many communities within Zapata County that fell victim to the rising waters of Falcon Lake as a result of the construction of Falcon Dam Reservoir in 1953. The Nuevo Santander Genealogy Society meets at the museum monthly.

Carrizo, and since 1898 as Zapata. This was one of twenty small hamlets and ranches founded north of the Rio Grande since 1750.

Visitors exploring the Rio Grande Valley Civil War Trail should begin their visit at the Zapata County Museum of History located at 805 North US Highway 83 in Zapata, Texas. In the museum you will find bilingual exhibits and a film that explore the natural and cultural history of the region. The Civil War figures prominently in the exhibition. Be certain to see the museum's recent acquisition—a light cavalry saber dating from 1864. The Zapata County Museum of History is open from 10:00 a.m. to 4:00 p.m., Tuesday through Friday (956-765-8983). Group tours are available by appointment on weekends. Allow a minimum of an hour for your visit; there is an admission fee.

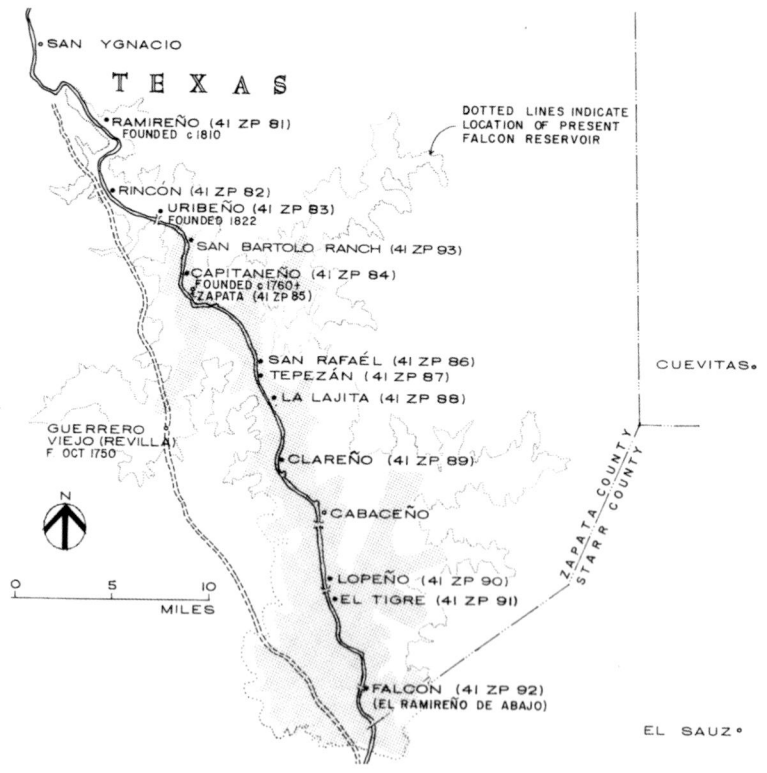

Figure 5.2. Map of Zapata County Texas region encompassed by present-day Falcon Lake to show location of ranches that have since been submerged when Falcon Dam was erected in 1953. Map courtesy of W. Eugene George, *Lost Architecture of the Rio Grande Borderlands*, Texas A&M University Press. To order this book, call (toll-free) 800–826–8911 or visit us online at www.tamupress.com.

Today, fourteen of the sites, including many of those most intimately associated with the American Civil War have, since 1953, been lost beneath the waters of Falcón International Reservoir. The residents of the historic towns were moved to new communities of the same historic name along Highway 83. Those traveling this route should pause at Falcón (Latitude 26° 38' 18.36" N Longitude 99° 05' 41.52" W), Lopeño (Latitude 26° 42' 40.27" N Longitude 99° 06'3 8.67" W), and Clareño Ranch (Latitude 26° 49' 03.60" N Longitude 99° 09' 31.92" W), and reflect on the submerged communities on both the Mexican and United States sides of the Rio Grande. Those interested in learning more about these communities should consult W. Eugene George's 2008 Texas A&M University Press book titled *Lost Architecture of the Rio Grande Borderlands*.

The remaining six sites are north of the reservoir bordering the Rio Grande. Some, like La Perla (Latitude 27° 11' 05.56" N Longitude 99°25'14.48" W), Los Corralitos Ranch (4744–4798, 5330 US 83 San Ygnacio, TX 78067; Latitude 27° 04' 33.91" N Longitude 99° 25' 44.47" W), and San Francisco (Latitude 27° 04' 57.29" N Longitude 99° 25' 46.79" W), are composed of a few buildings in various states of repair. Old Dolores, founded in 1750, is on private property and is inaccessible to visitors.

San Yganacio

One can still experience the flavor of the communities lost under the waters of Falcón International Reservoir at San Ygnacio, which was founded in 1830 (Latitude 27° 02' 38.18" N Longitude 99° 26'23.01" W). During the American Civil War, Confederate troops clashed here with followers of Juan Cortina.

San Ygnacio is today home to fewer than seven hundred people. It was here in 1952 that the Marlon Brando film *Viva Zapata!* was partially filmed. In 1972 San Ygnacio was listed on the National Register of Historic Places as the last example of nineteenth century Mexican Ranch vernacular architecture. Its oldest building in the community is the Treviño-Uribe Rancho. Built 1830, it is restored and is listed as a National Historic Landmark. Unfortunately, the site is not open to the public.

TEXAS HISTORICAL COMMISSION—HISTORICAL MARKER #13287
SAN YGNACIO

In the late 1820s, Jesus Treviño bought land and a hacienda from the heirs of José Vásquez Borrego. Treviño and his family, as well as several residents from nearby Revilla, Mexico (Guerrero), established a ranch and settlement and named it for Revilla's patron saint, San Ignacio de Loyola. In 1830, Treviño moved the ranch upriver, and for his headquarters he constructed a building of native sandstone. In 1851, his son-in-law, Blás María Uribe, had José Villarreal build and place a sundial on the entrance. Uribe later added other structures, forming the compound known today as Fort Treviño, or El Fuerte. Uribe also joined in discussions surrounding the formation of the Republic of the Río Grande. He and his brothers-in-law, Vicente Gutiérrez and Manuel Benavides García, were active leaders in San Ygnacio, which became a regional trade center, with access to land and river routes. In 1873, Uribe deeded land for Nuestra Señora del Refugio Catholic Church. Largely populated by

Figure 5.3. Treviño Fort, San Ygnacio, Texas, is on the National Register of Historic Places and is currently being renovated thanks to a grant provided by the National Park Service, along with local matching funds generated by the River Pierce Foundation. This structure, built in 1830, also known as the Treviño-Uribe Rancho, is located on a bluff above a point where the Rio Grande once flowed and is representative of typical colonial Mexican ranch architecture.

farmers and laborers, and following many years as a duty-free border zone, San Ygnacio continued to prosper late into the 19th century. The settlement, bypassed by the railroad in the 1880s, remained viable through its farming and ranching enterprises. Throughout the years, the area was often involved in political and military operations. In the early 1950s, plans for Falcon Reservoir posed a threat to the historic townsite. A committee headed by Mercurio Martínez successfully petitioned government officials to spare the community. Despite flood damage incurred in 1954, San Ygnacio has remained intact. Today, it is a unique example of a mid-19th century Texas border town, with numerous native sandstone structures, and is considered the oldest inhabited settlement in Zapata County (2005).

Access: This structure is undergoing restoration and is currently not open to the public.

TEXAS HISTORICAL COMMISSION—HISTORICAL MARKER #5556
JESUS TREVIÑO HOME

Jesus Trevino, founder of San Ygnacio, built this home in 1830, forting up family and neighbors here during frequent Indian raids. Later Blas Maria Uribe, his son-in-law, built the loopholed fort and in 1851 had a native stone made into a polished sundial and set into the north wall of the fort.

Location: Trevino and Uribe Avenues, San Ygnacio, TX

TEXAS HISTORICAL COMMISSION—HISTORICAL MARKER #3837
OLD ZAPATA

In 1770 residents of Revilla, Mexico, established a village (4.5 mi. W) on land granted by José de Escandón. The same year the Spanish built a fort nearby. In 1842 the men on the ill-fated expedition to Mier occupied the village while they foraged for supplies. First named "Habitacion," the town grew to be second largest on the Rio Grande. It was named for friendly Indians living in "carrizo" (cane) huts. In 1858, after Zapata County was created, the name changed to "Bellville" and then back to "Carrizo." In 1898 "Zapata" was chosen for Col. Antonio Zapata, a rancher executed for his part in the 1839 fight to found the Republic of the Rio Grande. Henry Redmond, a well-known area rancher, was the first county judge. Another county judge was Jose Antonio

George Navarro, son of Jose Antonio Navarro, one of the two native-born signers of the Texas Declaration of Independence. The elimination of duty free trade along the border in 1903 caused an economic decline. With the coming of irrigation, a rich agricultural area developed. After the construction of Falcon Dam and the flooding of Old Zapata by lake water, the county seat was relocated at this site on land originally granted to Bartolome Cuellar and Jacinto de Cuellar.

Location: US 83, Courthouse Grounds, Zapata, TX

Confrontation at Carrizo

On April 12, 1861, the American Civil War began at Fort Sumter in Charleston, South Carolina, and 1,400 miles away, in Zapata Country, Texas. Strong Unionist support existed in Zapata County from the earliest days of the Confederacy in Texas. An influential resident, Antonio Ochoa, rallied several Union supporters and confronted Zapata County Judge Isidro Vela in April 1861 at Carrizo, the county seat for Zapata County. Although the vote to join the Confederacy had been reported as unanimous by county officials, there were several prominent citizens who demanded that Zapata County remain within the Union. After a long meeting, Judge Vela persuaded Ochoa and his supporters to return peacefully to their homes.

    A mistrust of central authority was inherent in Zapata, borne from the principles of individual rights guaranteed by *El Fuero Juzgo*, the Spanish book of laws in effect since the sixth century, and manifested most prominently in the area through the actions of such important figures as Bernardo Gutiérrez de Lara, who had launched a strong challenge during the War of Independence against the Spanish authorities, declaring Texas independent in 1813. In 1839, in direct defiance to the dictatorial rule of President Antonio López de Santa Ana in Mexico City, Zapata County became the seminal center for the formation of La República del Río Grande, hosting the initial gathering of the leaders of the movement at the village of El Uribeño, where the republic was proclaimed. Such independence of mind and spirit would contribute to the conflicts in Zapata County during the US Civil War.

Location: Carrizo in Zapata County on the East Bank of the Río Grande at the confluence of the Río Salado and the Río Grande. Take US 83 toward Laredo from the Zapata County Museum of History. Turn left on 13th Avenue (FM

496) and turn left onto FM 3074. Follow that to the end of the pavement. It overlooks the site of the town.
Access: Currently submerged under Falcón International Reservoir. Please visit Zapata County Museum of History (Tuesday through Friday, 10:00 a.m. to 4:00 p.m.) for more information.
Rio Grande Valley Civil War Trail Mobile Web: 956-847-3002; **Extension:** 2602

Massacre at El Clareño
Several days after the April 1861 confrontation at Carrizo between Union supporters led by Antonio Ochoa and Zapata County Judge Isidro Vela, a Confederate Cavalry unit commanded by Capt. (later Col.) Santos Benavides, stationed in Laredo, arrived in Carrizo. Following Benavides's arrival, Judge Vela ordered Ochoa's arrest. Benavides and his unit proceeded to El Clareño, where Ochoa and his supporters lived. A battle ensued on April 15, in which nine were killed. The news of the massacre spread quickly throughout Zapata County and other communities on both sides of the border. The situation became more complicated as Unionist feelings were mixed with sympathy for Juan Cortina, a landowner from the Brownsville area, who was dispossessed of his lands by dishonest judges and attorneys. Such men had colluded with law enforcement officials who together coveted land grants in existence since Spanish colonial times. The deaths at El Clareño resulted in stronger local opposition to the Confederacy, as well as opposition to using the border area as an export base for cotton through Mexican ports in order to evade the Union Fleet blockade of Confederate ports.
Location: El Clareño was a small community in Zapata County dedicated to farming and ranching 15 miles south of Carrizo, the county seat for Zapata County.
GPS Coordinates: Latitude 26°46'04" N Longitude 99°14'16" W
Access: Currently submerged under Falcón International Reservoir. Please visit Zapata County Museum of History for more information.
Rio Grande Valley Civil War Trail Mobile Web: 956-847-3002; **Extension:** 2605

Figure 5.4. Ranch house found at El Clareño. Courtesy of the Texas Archeological Research Laboratory. TARL reference 41ZP89(4) (FR6, 35mm neg).

Skirmish at Redmond's Ranch

John Redmond's Ranch was located just south of the Zapata County seat of Carrizo (modern Zapata) in San Bartolo, on a property acquired from the Cuellar family, into which he had married. In 1858, Redmond, a local merchant and postmaster, had petitioned for the formation of Zapata County from lands in Webb and Starr counties. Within a short time, he became the first Zapata county judge and wielded significant political influence. On May 21, 1861, following Col. Santos Benavides's killings of Union supporters at El Clareño, a force of more than seventy Cortinistas—followers of Juan Cortina—surrounded a Confederate unit at Redmond's Ranch. Confederate reinforcements soon arrived from Laredo, causing Cortina to retreat across the Río Grande after a running fight. At the end of the Civil War the US Army, including US Colored Troops, created a post at this ranch that lasted until 1867.

Location: San Bartolo, TX, Zapata County

GPS Coordinates: Latitude 26°54'30.00" N Longitude 99°19'14.00" W

Access: Currently submerged under Falcón International Reservoir. Please visit Zapata County Museum of History (Tuesday through Friday, 10:00 a.m. to 4:00 p.m.) for more information.

Rio Grande Valley Civil War Trail Mobile Web: 956-847-3002; **Extension:** 2607

Confederate Retaliation at La Soledad

After the skirmish at Redmond's Ranch (San Bartolo) and the running battle at Carrizo (Old Zapata) in May 1861, Juan Cortina and his followers did not return to Zapata County. However, the fight against the Texas Confederates continued under the leadership of Octaviano Zapata. In December 1862, Zapata and his followers attacked a Confederate supply train near Roma, causing an interruption in the Confederate supply lines. The Confederates retaliated by destroying homes at La Soledad, a small farming and ranching community in Zapata County located about 10 miles south of Carrizo (Old Zapata). This retaliatory action inflicted further damage on relations between the Confederacy and its dissenters in Zapata County, leading to further turmoil.

Location: La Soledad was located about 10 miles south of Carrizo, the county seat for Zapata County near modern Arroyo Clareño, Texas 78076.

GPS Coordinates: Latitude 26° 48' 11.20" N Longitude 99° 15' 02.60" W

Access: Currently submerged under Falcón International Reservoir. Please visit Zapata County Museum of History (Tuesday through Friday, 10:00 a.m. to 4:00 p.m.) for more information.

Rio Grande Valley Civil War Trail Mobile Web: 956-847-3002; **Extension:** 2603

Second Battle of El Clareño and Hanging of Zapata County Judge

After the retaliatory attack of Confederate forces at La Soledad, in which houses and buildings were destroyed, Octaviano Zapata and his men attacked El Clareño, ultimately capturing and hanging Zapata County Judge Isidro Vela. Judge Vela was considered untrustworthy by Zapata and his followers after he issued orders to arrest Antonio Ochoa and his men, following an April 1861 meeting at Carrizo. Zapata and his men continued their raids along the border until September 1863, when Confederates under Maj. Santos Benavides crossed the Rio Grande and killed Zapata and several of his men near Mier, Tamaulipas, Mexico. Thereafter, the war moved away from Zapata County. Under the protection of Benavides's troops, area merchants and shippers were able to

Figure 5.5. Entrance to El Clareño Ranch property as seen from US Highway 83. This ranch is on private property and is not accessible to the public.

export Confederate cotton to Mexico for the lucrative European markets. In the process, they evaded the Union Navy's blockade of Confederate ports.

Location: El Clareño was a small community in Zapata County dedicated to farming and ranching 15 miles south of Carrizo, the county seat for Zapata County.

GPS Coordinates: Latitude 26° 46′ 04″ N Longitude 99° 14′ 16″ W

Access: Currently submerged under Falcón International Reservoir. Please visit Zapata County Museum of History (Tuesday through Friday, 10:00 a.m. to 4:00 p.m.) for more information.

Rio Grande Valley Civil War Trail Mobile Web: 956-847-3002; **Extension:** 2606

Reconstruction Era in Zapata County

The era of Reconstruction from 1865 to 1877 fostered political restrictions to Zapata County residents, as well as to those of all Texans. All elected officials had to submit their credentials to Governor Edmund J. Davis for review and approval prior to taking office. Cesáreo Flores was elected Sheriff of Zapata

Figure 5.6. Cesáreo Flores, sheriff of Zapata County, January 3, 1873. Courtesy of the Zapata County Museum of History.

County in 1872 but could not take the oath of office until Governor Davis issued a Certificate of Authorization attesting to his loyalty to the United States. Sheriff Flores's certificate from Governor Davis is dated January 3, 1873. Economically, Zapata, as well as other border towns, prospered greatly when Mexico's Juárez administration declared a duty-free zone all along its border with the United States. The tariff-free exchange of goods brought prosperity and modernization through the introduction of manufactured products that improved working and living conditions on the farms and ranches. During this period, the more affluent families began to send their children to schools in Laredo, San Antonio, Monterrey, and Saltillo. Also, many private schools began to open throughout the villages and towns of Zapata County, providing instruction to the population in general. Almost all instruction was conducted in Spanish, and the curriculum consisted of literature, reading, and arithmetic, with great emphasis on writing and penmanship, which was then recognized as a sign of personal refinement. Please visit Zapata County Museum of History for more information.

Rio Grande Valley Civil War Trail Mobile Web: 956–847–3002; **Extension:** 2608

WEBB
COUNTY
LAREDO
Clark Blvd.
Col. Santos Benavides Gravesite
Springfield Ave.
N. Meadow Ave.
Fort McIntosh
Washington St.
St. Augustine Plaza
Battle along Zacate Creek
59
35
83
359
359
N
S
E
W

6

Webb County Sites and Events

Laredo was founded by José de Escandón, as part of Nuevo Santander on the northern bank of the Rio Grande. It began as a small ranching community settled by Tomás Sánchez de la Barrera y Garza in 1755. In 1767 it was officially named the Villa de San Agustín de Laredo. Throughout the next century, the population slowly grew and, like most other villages along the river, was vulnerable to attack by Native American peoples. In 1821 when Mexico gained its independence from Spain, the town and surrounding land became part of the Mexican state of Tamaulipas. Largely excluded from events of the Texas Revolution in the 1830s, Laredo later became the capital of Republic of the Rio Grande in 1840 for a mere 282 tempestuous days. Six years later, prior to the termination of the Mexican-American War, Texas legislators included Laredo within the formation of Nueces County. In response to this peremptory action, the town's elite moved to remain part of Mexico, but with the signing of the Treaty of Guadalupe Hidalgo, the entire region north of the Rio Grande was annexed to the United States. As a result, many Laredoans moved across the river and established Nuevo Laredo. Webb County was formally established in January of 1848 in honor of Judge James Webb, who had served Texas in high political offices that included the Secretary of the Treasury, Secretary of State, and Attorney General.

By 1860, there were approximately 1,600 people living in Laredo, with an economy based largely on the selling of cattle and horses. During the course of the Civil War, the number of livestock in the county increased tenfold in response to the commercial needs of the Confederacy. As Confederate ports fell to the blockading Union Navy, the international border with Mexico became increasingly important for procuring war materials and money to fund the war. These years were known across the Rio Grande Valley as the "Cotton Times." Bales of cotton arrived at Eagle Pass, Laredo, Roma, Rio Grande City, and Brownsville by wagon from east Texas, Arkansas, and Louisiana. From these "port" towns, bales of cotton, or "white gold," were carried by steamboats or barges to Bagdad, Mexico. Once there, the bales were transferred to "lighters," small ships that could safely traverse the sandbar at the river's mouth to large ships waiting in the Gulf of Mexico.

When the Civil War began, Laredo was already a century old. The Benavides family, descendants of Tomás Sánchez de la Barrera y Garza, was one of the most prominent families in the community. Santos Benavides, a former mayor and county judge, and his two brothers, Refugio and Cristobal, served the Confederate cause in the 33rd Texas Cavalry (otherwise known as the Benavides Regiment) from 1861 to 1865. By November 1863, Santos Benavides was promoted to the rank of colonel. He was the highest ranking non-English-speaking soldier of Spanish descent in the Confederacy. In March 1864, the Benavides Regiment repulsed at Zacate Creek a force of two hundred men from the 1st Texas Cavalry seeking to capture or destroy five thousand bales of cotton awaiting export to Mexico. He and his regiment would also see action at Palmito Ranch in May of 1865, the last battle of the Civil War. The Benavides family is buried at Calvary Catholic Cemetery in Laredo.

When exploring the Rio Grande Valley Civil War Trail in Webb County, it is best to begin in the San Agustín de Laredo Historic District, which is framed by Iturbide, Santa Ursula, Convent, and Water Streets. Within that perimeter, you will find the Villa Antigua Border Heritage Museum (810 Zaragoza Street, 956-718-2727, open Tuesday through Saturday from 9:00 a.m. to 4:00 p.m., with admission fee) and the Republic of the Rio Grande Museum (1005 Zaragoza Street, 956-727-3480, open Tuesday through Saturday from 9:00 a.m. to 4:00 p.m., with admission fee). Both of these museums are run by the Webb County Heritage Foundation and are open to the public. The center of this historic district is St. Augustine Plaza, which is outlined by Zaragoza, Flores, San Agustín, and Grant Streets, anchored at the south end by the historic (and, yes, some say it is haunted!) La Posada Hotel (1000 Zaragoza Street, 956-722-1701, www.laposadahotel-laredo.com), which previously served as Laredo High School many years prior to its conversion into a hotel. The original Laredo High School was created in 1886 when the municipal building known as *Casa Consistoral* originally stood at this location. The school was torn down and rebuilt in 1917 and remained Laredo's main high school until Martin High School was built in 1937. Since 1961, La Posada Hotel has overlooked the square with its central park, gazebo, and multiple historic markers.

TEXAS HISTORICAL COMMISSION—1936 CENTENNIAL MARKER #15598
ORIGINAL SITE OF VILLA DE LAREDO
Original site of Villa de Laredo founded by Tomás Sánchez May 15, 1755 by order of José de Escandón colonizer of Nuevo Santander. Chartered by the King of Spain and organized as Villa de San Agustin de Laredo in 1767; Incorporated in the state of Tamaulipas, Mexico in 1821; Concentration point for the Mexican Army under General Santa Ana during the Texas Revolution; Capital of the Republic of the Rio Grande in 1839; Temporarily occupied by Texas by General Alexander Somervell in December 1842; Occupied November 8, 1846 for the United States by Captain Mirabeau B. Lamar under General Zachary Taylor; Incorporated as the City of Laredo by the Texas Legislature in 1848; Headquarters of Colonel Santos Benavides during the Confederacy; Ever after loyal to Old Glory.

Historic St. Augustine Plaza

St. Augustine Plaza is at the heart of a historic community established in 1755. In addition to the six flags that flew over Texas, Laredo had a seventh flag representing the Republic of the Rio Grande, an unsuccessful attempt to break with the Republic of Mexico in 1840. The capital of the Republic of the Rio Grande has been established as a museum and can be visited today on the south side of the plaza. During the Civil War, St. Augustine was a beehive of activity after Confederate officer Col. Santos Benavides established his headquarters there. Benavides's original home, along with that of his brother-in-law, John Z. Leyendecker, can be seen on the west side of the plaza. Most Confederate troops were garrisoned in buildings on or near the plaza for much of the war. Laredo became particularly important when cotton moved across the river, especially after the federal occupation of the Lower Rio Grande Valley in late 1863 and early 1864. For the citizens of Laredo, these were the "cotton times." Union forces attempted to destroy five thousand bales of cotton stacked in the plaza when they attacked the town in March 1864. Benavides and his men barricaded the streets with cotton bales and placed snipers on the buildings around the plaza. Although St. Augustine was largely treeless at the time, Benavides did manage to hang two horse thieves here during the war. A historical marker honoring the Benavides brothers, Santos, Refugio, and Cristobal, can be seen on the plaza today.

The perimeter of the plaza itself has shifted somewhat over time due to flooding of the Rio Grande during the past two-and-a-half centuries. The focal point of the plaza has always been St. Augustine Church. In 1755, the original church was a wattle-and-daub structure with a thatched roof known as a *jacal* and was located in the southeast corner of the square. The subsequent church building was a stone and adobe building that faced south. There is an outline of the foundation of this structure in the courtyard in front of the current church. The modern St. Augustine Cathedral dates from 1872. The school to the north of the church on the plaza was not standing during Civil War years. It was common practice in the late eighteenth century for priests or prominent citizens to be buried inside

Figure 6.1. Laredo Confederate soldiers from left to right: Refugio Benavides, Atanacio Vidaurri, Cristobal Benavides, and John Z. Leyendecker. Courtesy of Webb County Heritage Foundation.

Figure 6.2. John Z. Leyendecker's home stands on the southwest corner of St. Augustine Plaza, next to the original home of Colonel Santos Benavides.

the sanctuary of the church. It has been reported that Tomás Sánchez's gravesite is near the front of the school just outside the outline of the old church.

St. Augustine Plaza was used by Col. Benavides as his cavalry's headquarters throughout the American Civil War. It also is the location of his home. There are several structures on the square that were present in the 1860s. Santos Benavides's home, originally a two-story structure, and the home of his brother-in-law John Z. Leyendecker still stand next to each other on the west side of the square.

SIDEWALK MARKER
2ND CHURCH ON SAN AUGUSTÍN PLAZA
You are standing in the doorway of the 2nd church of San Augustín. The sandstone foundation which is outlined before you in tan brick was constructed in 1768 and is 18 inches below the surface. The church was built by the citizens of Laredo at the insistence of Governor González de Santiances of the Spanish province of Nuevo Santander. The mayor of Laredo at the time was Joseph Martínez de Sotomayor and the Priest was Fa. Nicolás Gutiérrez de Mendoza.

The first church of San Augustín was a small *jacal* on the southwest corner just behind you of the church property. It was built in 1755 as a missionary outpost until Fa. Juan José de Lafita y Verri was assigned as the first regular Priest for Laredo in 1762. Just inside the door before you is a small vestibule above which was the choir loft. Passing through the next door you enter the sanctuary and beyond this was the sacristy. The church was built of local sandstone with plastered and painted walls. At one time, the interior was wallpapered. The original hand-packed earthen floor was eventually paved with Spanish bricks. The building had the unusual proportions of 16 by 112 feet in size. It remained in use until 1872 when the present San Augustín church was dedicated.

TEXAS HISTORICAL COMMISSION—MARKER #367
BENAVIDES BROTHERS
Members of a prominent Laredo family, the three Benavides brothers were descendants of Tomás Sánchez, who founded the city in 1755. Santos (1823–91) and Refugio (born 1824) and their half-brother Cristobal (1839–1904) were best known for their service in the Confederate Army during the Civil War (1861–65). Santos commanded a regiment in the 33rd Texas Cavalry and rose to the rank of colonel, the highest rank achieved by a Mexican American in the Confederate Army. Both Refugio and Cristobal earned the rank of Captain. Stationed along the Texas-Mexico border, the brothers encountered both bandits and Union forces. In May 1862, they defeated a large raiding party led by Juan

Figure 6.3. This photo, taken in 1873, shows the newly built St. Augustine Church, with the original church still standing (facing south) toward the river. Plans for the construction of the new church began just after the US Civil War in 1866. Courtesy of the Ursuline Sisters Collection, Webb County Heritage Foundation.

Figure 6.4. Modern-day St. Augustine Cathedral built in 1872.

Cortina at Carrizo (now Zapata). In March 1864, although their troops were badly outnumbered, they defended Laredo against an army of Texas Unionists. Their victory helped ensure continuation of the vital Confederate cotton trade between Texas and Mexico. The Benavides brothers also distinguished themselves as political, commercial, and social leaders in Laredo. Santos and Cristobal operated one of the city's most prosperous mercantile companies. Santos also served in the state legislature, 1879–84. (1976)

Location: St. Augustine Plaza—within perimeter of Zaragoza, Flores, San Agustín, and Grant Streets, Laredo, TX 78040
GPS Coordinates: Latitude 27° 30' 08.20" N Longitude 99° 30' 20.57" W
Access: Public plaza
Rio Grande Valley Civil War Trail Mobile Web: 956–847–3002; **Extension:** 2805

Casa Ortiz

On the southeast corner of St. Augustine Plaza is a historic home, beautifully restored and maintained by Texas A&M International University in partnership with the Webb County Heritage Foundation. This structure was constructed by Jose Reyes Ortiz in 1830 with a lush interior courtyard. It is located directly across the street from St. Augustine Church and has the best view of the Rio Grande and Mexico.
Location: 915 Zaragoza Street, Laredo, TX 78040
GPS Coordinates: Latitude: 27° 30' 7.088" N Longitude: 99° 30' 18.73" W
Access: Open to the public Monday through Friday from 8:00 a.m. to 5:00 p.m., or by appointment
Admission Fee: None
Contact: 956–326–3200

Benavides Brothers
Santos Benavides

Col. Santos Benavides became the highest ranking Tejano to serve the Confederacy. Born in Laredo in 1823, he was a descendant of Tomás Sánchez de la Barrera y Garza, the founder of the small community. As a political and military leader in Laredo, Benavides brought a traditionally isolated region closer to the mainstream of Texas politics while preserving a sense of local independence. Assigned to the Rio Grande Military District at the beginning of the war, Benavides drove his rival Juan Cortina into Mexico at the battle of Carrizo in May 1861. He crushed other local revolts against Confederate authority on the Rio Grande. In November 1863 Benavides was authorized to raise his own force that became known simply as the Benavides Regiment. Perhaps his greatest triumph came on March 19, 1864, when he drove back more than two hundred soldiers from the Texas Union Cavalry. Benavides helped make possible the safe passage of cotton across the Rio Grande to Mexico during the Union occupation of the Lower Rio Grande Valley in 1863–64. During Reconstruction, Benavides remained active in his mercantile and ranching activities along with his brother Cristobal. He served three times in the Texas House of Representatives from 1879 to 1884, the only Tejano in the legislature at that time, and twice served as alderman in Laredo. He died at his home in Laredo in 1891 (see fig. 1.7).

TEXAS HISTORICAL COMMISSION—MARKER #4589
SANTOS BENAVIDES
Santos Benavides, son of José Jesus and Marguerita Benavides and great-great grandson of Laredo founder Tomás Sánchez, was born in Laredo on November 1, 1823. He married Augustina Villareal in 1842. Benavides, appointed *procurador* (administrative agent) of Laredo in 1843, openly cooperated with the forces of Mirabeau B. Lamar which occupied Laredo during the Mexican War (1846–48) in an effort to pacify the region. He was elected mayor of Laredo in 1856 and 1857 and chief justice of Webb County in 1859. During the Civil War Benavides raised a company of cavalry at Laredo which defeated Juan Cortina in the Battle of Carrizo in 1861. He became a colonel in command of his own regiment known as Benavides' Regiment. On March 19, 1864, his regiment successfully defended Laredo with only 42 men against a Union force of more than 200 men. During the late 1860s and 1870s, Benavides engaged in mercantile and ranching activities with his brother Cristobal. He served in the Texas Legislature during the 1880s and in 1884 was appointed Texas Commissioner to the world's Cotton Exposition. Benavides helped found the Guarache party, a faction of Laredo's Democratic Party. He died in Laredo on November 9, 1891. Sesquicentennial of Texas Statehood 1845–1995.

Rio Grande Valley Civil War Trail Mobile Web: 956–847–3002; **Extension:** 2803

TEXAS HISTORICAL COMMISSION—MARKER #4320
REFUGIO BENAVIDES
A native of Laredo, José Del Refugio Benavides was a descendant of Tomás Sánchez, who founded the city in 1755. As a member of one of Laredo's most celebrated families, he was instrumental in the city's development dur-

ing the 19th century. He was elected to the office of alderman in 1850 and mayor in 1859. During the Civil War Benavides and his brothers were active in defenses along the Texas-Mexico border. Rising to the rank of Captain, Refugio Benavides commanded a company in the 33rd Texas cavalry. His actions in defending the border against invasions by union troops and Mexican raiders led by Juan Cortina helped retain the Valley's important role as a vital cotton-exporting site for the Confederacy. In 1873, following Reconstruction, Refugio Benavides was again elected mayor of Laredo and served three successive terms. Among the accomplishments of his political career were improved public schools, city sewage systems, and the revision of the city charter. Married twice, Benavides was the father of six children. He died in 1899 and was buried in the Old Catholic Cemetery. He was reinterred here during World War II.

Figure 6.5. Cristobal Benavides cenotaph in the Benavides Family plot at Calvary Catholic Cemetery, Laredo, Texas.

Figure 6.6. Headstones of Colonel Santos Benavides, Captain Cristobal Benavides, and Captain Refugio Benavides at Calvary Catholic Cemetery, Laredo, Texas.

Location: Calvary Catholic Cemetery, 3600 McPherson Avenue, Laredo, TX 78040
GPS Coordinates: Latitude 27° 31′ 43.25″ N Longitude 99° 29′ 04.15″ W
Access: Open daily, 7:00 a.m. to 5:45 p.m.
Contact: 956-723-6811
Interesting Facts: The cemetery office only has records of burials from March 1917 to present day. All records prior to March 1917 would be found within the St. Augustine Cathedral archives.

Battle along Zacate Creek

With the Union occupation of the Lower Rio Grande Valley in late 1863 and early 1864, cotton from as near as East Texas and as far as Arkansas and Louisiana was diverted to Laredo and Eagle Pass for transport to Mexico. In March 1864, a small federal army left the Lower Valley, intent on seizing or destroying the large amount of cotton reported to be stacked in St. Augustine Plaza, Laredo. About half of the expedition was composed of members of the 2nd Texas Union Cavalry, a predominantly Tejano regiment. This Union force of more than two hundred men slowly advanced upriver. On March 19, 1864, one of Confederate colonel Santos Benavides's men spotted the advancing federals outside of Laredo. Benavides rallied his small Confederate force, barricaded several of the streets with cotton, and placed snipers on the buildings around St. Augustine Plaza. In all, Benavides could only field seventy-two men. At 3:00 p.m., when the federals dismounted and advanced, a furious firefight erupted that lasted for more than three hours. Three times the federals advanced, and three times they were driven back. Unable to seize the village in the growing darkness, the Union soldiers rapidly withdrew some two miles downriver and went into camp for the evening. Union casualties are uncertain, but several bloody rags were found along the banks of Zacate Creek and scattered in the scrubby mesquite. None of Benavides' defenders were killed or wounded.

Location: Battle at Zacate Creek—closest visible area from overpass on Iturbide Street as it turns into Market Street, Laredo, TX 78040
GPS Coordinates: Latitude 27° 30′ 18.04″ N Longitude 99° 29′ 46.54″ W
Access: Public property
Rio Grande Valley Civil War Trail Mobile Web: 956-847-3002; **Extension:** 2802

Arroyo Secate, two miles below Loredo.

Figure 6.7. This exaggerated sketch of Zacate Creek shows wagons moving toward Laredo in 1850. United States and Mexican Boundary Survey.

Figure 6.8. Zacate Creek view from south to north.

155

Fort McIntosh

Fort McIntosh was established in a bend of the Rio Grande less than a mile above Laredo on March 3, 1849, just below a favorite Indian crossing on the river called Paso de los Indios. Originally named Camp Crawford, it was later renamed in honor of Lt. Col. James Simmons McIntosh, who died of wounds received during the Mexican-American War. Nine of the nineteen men who commanded the isolated post in the years prior to the Civil War became generals during the Civil War. These include Union generals Philip H. Sheridan and Randolph B. Marcy, and for the Confederacy, James E. Slaughter. With the secession of Texas in 1861, the small garrison of federal troops departed Laredo, and Charles Callahan, agent for the state of Texas, took possession of the post. Shortly thereafter, it was turned over to Col. Santos Benavides, who moved his headquarters there from St. Augustine Plaza. However, early in the war, most of the buildings were sold by town authorities, and by 1865, there was little left of the original post. When the US Army, including US Colored Troops, reoccupied the property in 1865, Fort McIntosh was rebuilt and continued as one of the major posts on the Rio Grande. It was officially deactivated after World War II. The property was turned over to the local school district, which established a community college on the site. Many of the buildings, including one of the barracks dating to the 1880s, can be seen at Laredo Community College today.

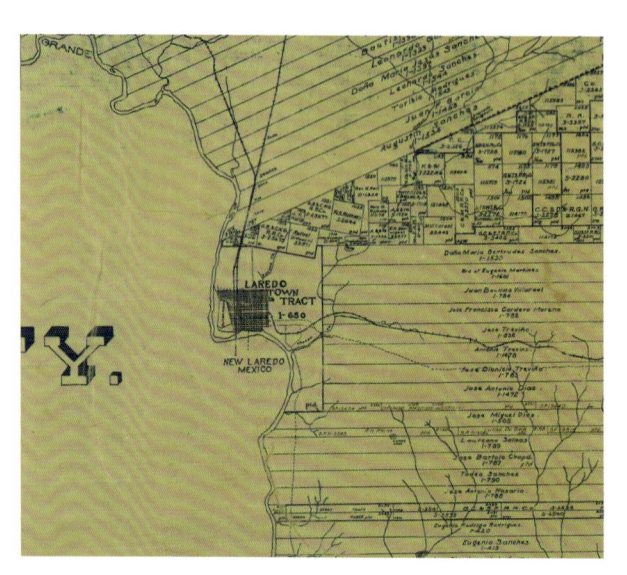

Figure 6.9. Webb County map of Laredo, with Fort McIntosh and Zacate Creek inset drawn by Tom G. Atlee, 1933. Courtesy of the Texas General Land Office, map no. 82053.

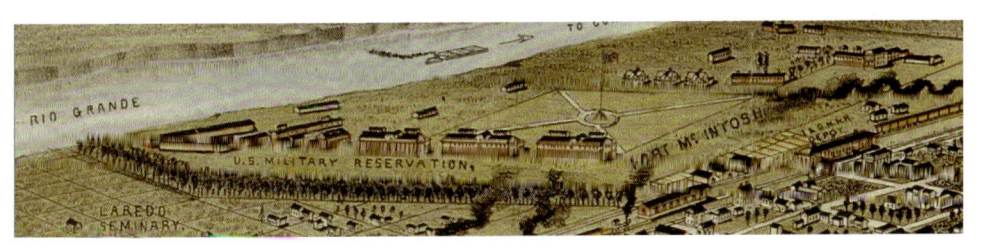

Figure 6.10. Fort McIntosh US Military Reservation, 1892.

After Fort Ringgold, the structures still standing at Fort McIntosh are the second largest extant group of military buildings that exist today on the Rio Grande Valley Civil War Trail. The historic buildings represent three waves of construction with different styles: those built by US Colored Troops in the late 1860s immediately following the end of the US Civil War, which includes the Bakery, the Company Storehouse, and the Post Hospital; those built during the post-Reconstruction period in 1885, such as the Officers' Quarters, the Commanding Officer's Quarters, and the Post Guardhouse; and those built in 1905 at the turn of the twentieth century, such as the Enlisted Men's Barracks building.

Location: Fort McIntosh, West End Washington Street at Laredo Community College, Laredo, TX 78040

GPS Coordinates: Latitude 27° 30′ 30.24″ N, 99° 31′ 09.19″ W

Access: Visitors are welcome to explore the historic site every day during daylight hours but need to arrange with the college's Public Relations Office. Visitors may enter the chapel, built in 1895 to serve the camp's religious needs. Visitors may also enter building #P34/P35, built in 1885 to serve as Officers' Quarters. All other structures are limited to external viewing only.

Contact: Public Relations Office: 956–721–5140; Email contact: mpro@laredo.edu

Rio Grande Valley Civil War Trail Mobile Web: 956–847–3002; **Extension:** 2804

Figure 6.11. Fort McIntosh Bakery, built in 1869 by USCT during Reconstruction.

Figure 6.12. Company Storehouse, built in 1868 by USCT during Reconstruction.

Figure 6.13. Post Hospital at Fort McIntosh, built in 1868 by USCT during Reconstruction.

Figure 6.14. Commanding Officer's Quarters, 1885, at Fort McIntosh, which now serves as the home of the president of Laredo Community College.

Figure 6.15. Officers' Quarters at Fort McIntosh, built in 1885, which now serves as the Public Relations and Marketing Office at Laredo Community College.

Figure 6.16. Post Guardhouse, built in 1886, as it stands today at Laredo Community College.

Figure 6.17. Former barracks at Fort McIntosh (built 1905), which now serve as Arechiga Hall of Laredo Community College.

Further Reading

Guerra, Maria Eugenia. *Historic Laredo: An Illustrated History of Laredo and Webb County*. San Antonio: Historical Publishing Network, 2001.

Thompson, Jerry. *Laredo: A Pictorial History*, Norfolk: The Donning Company Publishers, 1986.

7

US Colored Troops

As Southern states such as Texas seceded from the United States prior to the onset of the US Civil War, the main conflict between the North and the South was clear. The Northern states favored industry and central government control, which was in stark contrast to the Southern population's preference for a more agrarian, libertarian, and racially hierarchical society. Southerners wanted the right to continue exploiting the labor of their slaves and feared the loss of profits and autonomy if the Northern method of governing ruled the land. Although it is a common perception that slavery was the sole cause and/or purpose of the US Civil War, it must be clarified that initially President Abraham Lincoln specifically excluded its abolition as an agenda item for his administration. In fact, the Emancipation Proclamation was issued by executive order on January 1, 1863, halfway through the war itself. Moreover, it applied only to slaves in territories in active rebellion against the United States, which excluded many slaves who lived in states that had not seceded. That being the case, it may be more accurate to say not that the war was fought to free the slaves, but that the slaves were emancipated in order for the Union to win the war. Initially the intention was to placate Lincoln's domestic political critics and undermine Confederate efforts to win diplomatic support in Great Britain and elsewhere. But an even more direct advantage for the Union came when Lincoln suggested and the War Department implement General Order No. 143, which allowed emancipated slaves to be conscripted into the US Army.

Lincoln had the insight that black men would make good soldiers. As he observed early in 1863 in a letter to Andrew Johnson, "The colored population is the great *available* yet *unavailed*-of force for restoring the Union." With rising casualties depleting the ranks of the conventional army, this infusion of black soldiers had the potential for changing the entire course of the war. The US Army XXV Corps of the US Colored Troops (USCT) was created in Virginia during the latter part of the Civil War and was the only corps composed entirely of black enlisted men, forming the umbrella under which all US Colored Troops served. This addition of nearly 180,000 men constituted 10–15 percent of total Union manpower during the last two years of the war, providing the Union with what Lincoln had hoped: sufficient manpower to ensure victory.

Three regiments of the USCT entered the Rio Grande Valley in the fall of 1864 under the command of Maj. Gen. Godfrey Weitzel and remained encamped at Brazos Santiago for the war's duration. The majority of men serving in these regiments consisted of those who originally enlisted at Camp Nelson in Kentucky, such as the 114th, 116th, 117th, and 118th US Colored Infantries. Additionally, the 62nd Regiment of USCT mustered into service in Missouri in December 1863 and arrived at Brazos Santiago also in the fall of 1864. A detachment of the 62nd Infantry fought Confederates at the Battles of Palmito Ranch on May 12–13 and at White's Ranch on May 13, 1865. Two weeks later, on May 30, the 62nd, along with other US Army units, moved into Brownsville. By May 1865, nearly 16,000 USCT veterans of the XXV Corps arrived at Brazos Santiago from City Point, Virginia, and were quickly dispersed to Forts Brown at Brownsville, Ringgold Barracks at Rio Grande City, Fort McIntosh at Laredo, and Fort Duncan at Eagle Pass along the river. Once the US Civil War was over, the mission of these regiments was to keep the peace in the region and to guard against illicit smuggling and protect the international border. They were also tasked to make sure that rogue Confederates, who had crossed the river into Mexico to regroup and rearm themselves after the surrender of Gen. Robert E. Lee, were not successful in crossing back over the Rio Grande to resume their fight and attack the Union. And while they had to appear to be neutral with respect to the goings on in Mexico, they were nonetheless a threatening presence in support of Benito Juárez's Liberal forces there as he sought to defeat French and Austrian Imperial forces under Emperor Maximilian, an unstated yet significant aim for American foreign policy. The last USCT regiment, the 117th US Colored Infantry, left the Rio Grande in July 1867.

Figure 7.1. Photograph shows a view of Levee Street in Brownsville, Texas, from the pontoon bridge constructed by United States forces across the Rio Grande from Matamoros, Mexico, in November of 1866. The bridge is guarded by armed sentries of the 114th US Colored Infantry. Library of Congress.

Figure 7.2. Private William Wright, 114th US Colored Infantry. Courtesy of Ron Coddington.

Even though this would appear to mean that the black military presence ended just two years after the end of the US Civil War (i.e. only during the earlier phase of the Reconstruction era), African American soldiers and their regiments continued to occupy the military forts along the Rio Grande. The USCT was disbanded; however, they were replaced by regular US regiments consisting of former USCT troops and other black recruits. Those who came to man the border posts were the 9th US Cavalry and the 41st US Infantry, later referred to as Buffalo Soldiers. With the arrival of the 24th and 25th Infantries toward the end of the 1860s, there were approximately two thousand black soldiers stationed at military forts along the border between El Paso and Brownsville. For the next forty years, their purpose was to continue the tradition of protecting the US border and the frontier region more generally against cross-border violence and Native American incursions. These black soldiers made a fine adjustment to the hot desert terrain and diverse culture of the Valley, as explained by Sgt. Maj. Thomas Boswell of the 116th: "If our regiment stays here any length of time, we will all speak Spanish, as we are learning very fast."[1]

Palmito Ranch Battlefield

Location: 12 miles east of Brownsville on Texas Highway 4 (Boca Chica Boulevard), 43794 Palmito Hill Road. Brownsville, Texas, 78521. Do not miss the wayside exhibits located just off Highway 4 on Palmito Hill Road.
GPS Coordinates: Latitude 25° 57′ 37.72″ N Longitude 97° 18′ 08.83″ W
Access: 8:00 a.m. to 5:00 p.m. No facilities are available. Administered by the US Fish and Wildlife Service.
Rio Grande Valley Civil War Trail Mobile Web: 956–847–3002; **Extension:** 2017

PROPOSED TEXAS HISTORICAL COMMISSION MARKER (PENDING APPROVAL)
UNITED STATES COLORED TROOPS
The last land battle of the Civil War was fought in Texas on May 12–13, 1865, at Palmetto Ranch in Cameron County and some 16,000 United States Colored Troops participated in that battle.

---

1. Quoted from Edwin S. Redkey, ed., *A Grand Army of Black Men: Letters from African-American Soldiers in the Union Army, 1861–1865* (New York: Cambridge University Press, 1992), 203.

The United States Colored Troops likewise played a decisive role in the Civil War, comprising ten percent of the Union Army and twenty-five percent of the Union Navy.

In July of 1862, Congress passed the Militia Act of 1862. It had become an "indispensable military necessity" to call on America's African descent population to help save the Union. A few weeks after President Lincoln signed the legislation on July 17, 1862, free men of color joined volunteer regiments in Illinois and New York. Such men would go on to fight in some of the most noted campaigns and battles of the war to include, Antietam, Vicksburg, Gettysburg, and Sherman's Atlanta Campaign.

By the end of 1863, General Ulysses S. Grant viewed the African descent population armed with the [Emancipation] Proclamation as a "powerful ally."

Lincoln recognized their contributions, declaring, "Without the military help of the black freedmen, the war against the South could not have been won." And without the Emancipation Proclamation, these soldiers and sailors would have had little reason to fight for the Union.

The Federal blockade was applied to the Texas coast early in July 1861. By 1863 almost eight thousand federal troops were planted on Texas soil. The struggle for control of the Rio Grande Valley and in the fight at Palmetto Ranch emphasize the international and intercultural nature of Texas' southernmost region.

By May 1865, nearly 16,000 USCT veterans of the 25th Corps arrived at Brazos Santiago from City Point, Virginia, and were quickly dispersed to Forts Brown at Brownsville, Ringgold Barracks at Rio Grande City, Fort McIntosh at Laredo, and Fort Duncan at Eagle Pass, as well as to smaller posts where they were assigned to prevent former Confederates from establishing their defeated government and army in Mexico....The last USCT regiment, the 117th US Colored Infantry, left the Rio Grande in July 1867.

Camp Nelson Civil War Heritage Park

Those interested in the USCT who served along the Rio Grande may want to plan an out-of-state trip to Nicolasville, Kentucky, about twenty-five miles south of Lexington. Kentucky, a slave state, did not join the Confed-

eracy. In 1863, following the Emancipation Proclamation, thousands of formerly enslaved African Americans made their way to Kentucky. There, three thousand of these "Contraband," as the ex-slaves were known, helped construct Camp Nelson, a Union recruitment and training center in 1863. Here, beginning in 1864 and continuing to the end of the war, ten thousand African Americans were emancipated in exchange for service in the Union Army. There were two other training camps for the US Colored Troops in New Orleans and Camp Meigs in Readville outside Boston. The latter is best remembered for the 54th Regiment Massachusetts Volunteer Infantry, featured in the 1989 film *Glory*. Today Camp Nelson, in rural Kentucky, is the only surviving training camp associated with the USCT.
Location: 6614 Danville Road, Nicholasville, KY 40356
GPS Coordinates: Latitude 37°47′23.11″ N Longitude 84°36′27.57″ W
Access: Open Tuesday through Saturday, 9:00 a.m. to 5:00 p.m.
Admission Fee: None
Contact: 859-881-5716

Buffalo Soldiers National Museum
African American soldiers have served in the armies of the United States since the American Revolution. During the American Civil War and Reconstruction eras, segregated regiments of African American troops served widely in Texas. The Army Reorganization Act of July 28, 1866, created six all African American army units. The units were identified as the 9th and 10th Cavalry and the 38th, 39th, 40th, and 41st Infantry Regiments. The four infantry regiments were later reorganized to form the 24th and 25th Infantry Regiments. At the Battle of Palmito Ranch in May of 1865, the 62nd US Colored Infantry served with distinction. Following the war, African American troops served at Forts Brown, Ringgold, McIntosh, and Duncan along the Rio Grande, and at other posts in Texas and beyond.
Location: 3816 Caroline Street, Houston, TX 77004
Access: Monday through Saturday: 10:00 a.m. to 4:00 p.m.
Admission Fee: Yes (please contact site for current fee structure)
Contact: 713-942-8920; www.buffalosoldiermuseum.com

Figure 7.3. Buffalo Soldiers National Museum, Houston.

Figure 7.4. Bronze sculpture of Buffalo Soldier at Buffalo Soldiers National Museum, Houston.

Given the ubiquitous nature of African American military soldiers in the Rio Grande Valley region and the significance of their service, we have listed here their regiments and the locations occupied by them throughout the Civil War era.

Cameron County US Colored Troops: Civil War Station Locations

Brazos Santiago

Post occupied by the US Army from Fall 1863 through the end of the Civil War and after. Occupied by USCT in the Fall of 1864, including the 62nd, 87th, and 91st USCI. Staging point for the campaign toward Palmito Ranch in May 1865. Later, June 1865–67, primary landing point by USCT under the XXV Corps, District of the Rio Grande. These USCT built a railroad from here to White's Ranch in late 1865.

Figure 7.5. Map of US Military Railroad from Brazos Santiago to Whites Ranche [sic], Texas, in 1866. Brazos Santiago Depot is shown with military quarantine hospital on Dyers Island and campsites of the 81st US Colored Infantry and 34th Indiana Volunteers.

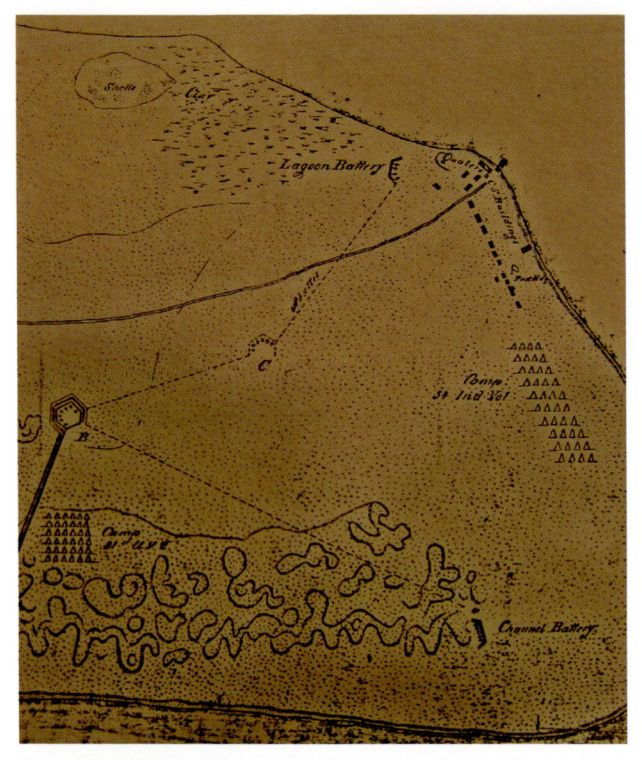

Figure 7.6. Enlarged section of Map of US Military Railroad from Brazos Santiago to Whites Ranche [sic] to show segregated campsites of the 81st US Colored Infantry (87th and 95th) and 34th Indiana Volunteers.

Clarksville, Texas

Post of USCT, XXV Corps, District of the Rio Grande, 1865–67. Occupied by companies of the 45th, 46th, and 118th USCI and 2nd USCC, among others. Point of departure for two movements into Bagdad, Mexico, July 1865 (45th) and January 1866 (46th, 118th, 2nd) in support of Liberal forces.

Fort Brown

Major post on the Rio Grande. Occupied by US Army November 1863–July 1864 and again after May 30, 1865. HQ of XXV Corps (Maj. Gen. Godfrey Weitzel) and District of the Rio Grande (Maj. Gen. Frederick Steele), June 1865–67. Garrisoned by various USCT regiments, including the 19th and

Figure 7.7. Fort Brown guardhouse manned by USCT. DeGolyer Library, Southern Methodist University, Lawrence T. Jones III Texas Photographs.

114th USCI, who built a pontoon bridge across the river and invaded Matamoros in November–December 1866.

Palmito Ranch
Site of May 12–13, 1865, Civil War battle between US forces under Col. Theodore Barrett (62nd USCI, 34th Indiana Infantry, and 2nd Texas Cavalry) and Confederate forces under Col. John S. "Rip" Ford. The battle was a Confederate victory, with numerous US soldiers captured and the majority returning to Brazos Santiago.

White's Ranch
Encampment of the 62nd and 84th USCI, 34th Indiana Infantry, and 2nd Texas Cavalry (US) on their march toward Palmito Ranch (May 9–10, 1865). Post for USCT, XXV Corps, District of the Rio Grande, June 1865–67. These troops built a railroad line from here to Brazos Santiago (December 1865). The 116th USCI suffered from a Cholera epidemic here in August 1866, which "destroyed the lives of forty-five men."

Various Smaller Sites: Arenal and Santa Maria
These ranches were all small posts for USCT companies from 1865–67. Companies of the 116th USCI at Arenal and Santa Maria.

Figure 7.8. Flag representing US Colored Infantry 84th Regiment station locations. Note White Ranche, Texas, May 1865. Courtesy of the Behring Center—Smithsonian Institution.

Hidalgo County US Colored Troops: Station Locations
Edinburgh, Texas (City of Hidalgo)
Post of USCT under XXV Corps, District of the Rio Grande, June 1865–67. Various regiments/companies stationed here, including Companies A, D, H, and K of the 116th USCI (fall 1865) and Co. G of the 114th USCI (spring 1866).

Starr County US Colored Troops: Station Locations
Ringgold Barracks, Texas
Major post of USCT, XXV Corps, District of the Rio Grande from June 1865

to 1867. Regimental HQ of the 114th USCI (spring 1866; winter–spring 1867). Last post of last USCT (117th USCI) in Rio Grande Valley–left July 1867 and replaced by the 41st US Infantry.

Roma, Texas
Post for USCT, XXV Corps, District of the Rio Grande, June 1865–67. Regimental HQ for 116th USCI, summer 1865, and post for companies of 31st and 114th USCI. In August 1865, four companies of 116th and 31st pursued Kickapoo raiding party from Mexico.

Zapata County US Colored Troops: Station Locations
Various Smaller Sites: Barrancas, Cortina, Redmond's, and Santa Maria Ranches
These ranches were all small posts for USCT companies from 1865 to 1867. Companies of the 114th USCI at Redmond's Ranch

Webb County US Colored Troops: Station Locations
Fort McIntosh, Texas
Major post of USCT, XXV Corps, District of the Rio Grande from June 1865 to 1867. Companies A and I of the 114th USCI were here spring 1866. In July 1867, occupied by companies of the 41st US Infantry. Companies F and G of the 117th USCI, 1866–67.

8

Beyond the Rio Grande Valley Civil War Trail

Exploring the American Civil War in Texas and Mexico

The Rio Grande Valley Civil War Trail encompasses only a portion of locations in Texas associated with the American Civil War. Those interested in visiting other sites are encouraged to consult Thomas E. Alexander and Dan K. Utley's 2012 book, titled *Faded Glory: A Century of Forgotten Texas Military Sites, Then and Now*, and the Texas Historical Commission's 2002 brochure, *Texas in the Civil War: Stories of Sacrifice, Valor and Hope*. These include a cross-section of sites that illuminate this important era in the history of Texas. These include ranches, museums, forts, POW camps, battlefields, and Confederate veterans' reunion grounds.

King Ranch

Established as the Santa Gertrudis Ranch in 1853, the King Ranch had almost 150,000 acres at the time of the Civil War. Its founder, Richard King, contracted with the Confederacy to provide supplies to soldiers in return for overseeing cotton smuggling through the Union blockade. Besides the Santa Gertrudis Ranch, the King family had business enterprises in Brownsville and Rio Grande City. A Confederate camp, San Fernando, was established nearby in June 1863 to protect the cross-border trade. The main house of the ranch

Figure 8.1. Captain Richard King. Courtesy of King Ranch Archives.

Figure 8.2. Santa Gertrudis House on the King Ranch 1860. Courtesy of King Ranch Archives.

was occupied by Union troops in December of 1863. Following the war, King was pardoned after taking a loyalty oath to the United States, and the ranch was returned to his control.

To learn more about Richard King and the King Ranch, visit the King Ranch Museum in Kleberg County.

Location: 405 North 6th Street, Kingsville, TX 78363
Access: Monday through Saturday: 10:00 a.m. to 4:00 p.m.; Sunday 1:00 p.m. to 5:00 p.m.
Admission Fee: Yes
Contact: 361-595-1881; https://king-ranch.com/museum/
Rio Grande Valley Civil War Trail Mobile Web: 956-847-3002; **Extension:** 2902

Texas Civil War Museum

Texas Civil War Museum, located at 760 Jim Wright Freeway North in Fort Worth, Texas, is the largest Civil War Museum west of the Mississippi River. There, visitors will see Union and Confederate infantry, cavalry, artillery, naval, and medical uniforms and associated accoutrements. Of special interest to those interested in the Rio Grande theatre of the Civil War are artifacts from the Palmito Ranch battlefield and a 1/32nd scale diorama of the battle built

Figure 8.3. Texas Civil War Museum in Fort Worth.

Figure 8.4. Diorama of the last land battle of the US Civil War at Palmito Ranch created by students at Highland High School in Gilbert, Arizona. Note the US Colored Troops in the foreground. Courtesy of the Texas Civil War Museum, Fort Worth.

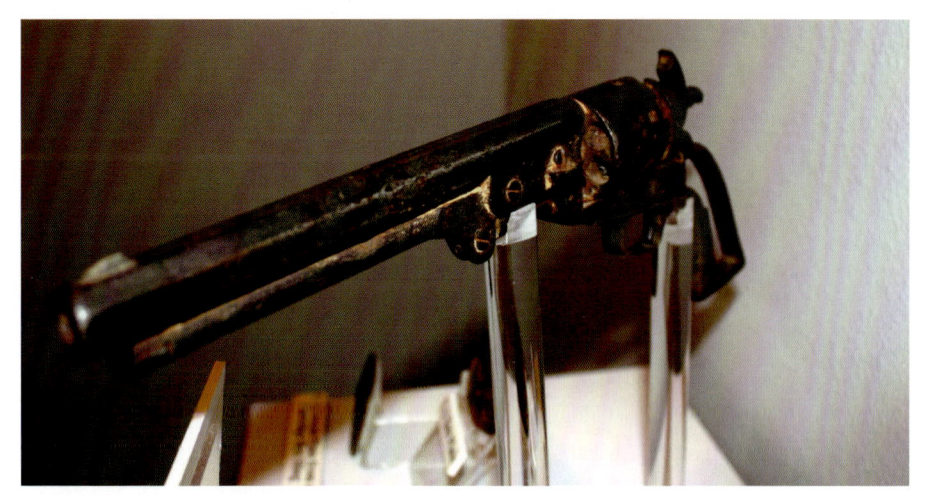

Figure 8.5. Pistol found at Palmito Ranch Battlefield. Courtesy of Texas Civil War Museum, Fort Worth. Note that the pistol is still cocked, loaded, and ready to fire.

by students at Highland High School in Gilbert, Arizona. The construction depicts the 62nd US Colored Infantry and the 34th Indiana Infantry Regiment doing battle with the 33rd Confederate Texas Cavalry Regiment commanded by Cols. John S. Ford and Santos Benavides. In the background, onlookers watch the battle from a Mexican-flagged steamboat owned by Richard King and Mifflin Kenedy.

Location: 760 Jim Wright Freeway North, Fort Worth, TX 76108
GPS Coordinates: Latitude: 32° 46′ 20.68″ N, Longitude: 97° 28′ 26.95″ W
Access: Tuesday through Saturday: 9:00 a.m. to 5:00 p.m.
Admission Fee: Yes (please contact site for current fee structure)
Contact: 817–246–3951; www.texascivilwarmuseum.com

Forts

Military establishments were widely founded in the fifteen years leading up to the American Civil War. These included Forts Duncan (1849), Belknap (1851), Mason (1851), Phantom Hill (1852), McKavett (1852), Chadbourne (1852), Bliss (1854), Davis (1854), Lancaster (1855), and Stockton (1859), to name a few. These saw Union and later Confederate occupations. In the fall of 1861, Gen. Henry H. Sibley led an army from San Antonio to Fort Bliss, and from this staging point invaded the New Mexico Territory in February 1862, where they fought and defeated Union forces at Valverde on February 21, but a month later following the Battle of Glorieta Pass on March 28, were forced to retreat to Texas (Alexander and Utley 2012: 59–65).

A number of these frontier forts are preserved and interpreted. These include Fort Bliss (open Monday through Saturday, 10:00 a.m. to 3:00 p.m.; free admission; located on Marshall Road, Fort Bliss, TX 79916; http://www.bliss.army.mil/Museum/fort_bliss_museum.htm; 915–568–4512), Fort McKavett State Historic Site (open daily, 8:00 a.m. to 5:00 p.m.; admission fee; located in Menard County at 7066 FM 864, Fort McKavett, TX 76841; 325–396–2358), and Fort Davis National Historic Site (open daily, 8:00 a.m. to 5:00 p.m.; admission fee; located at 101 Lt. Flipper Drive #1379 Fort Davis, TX 79734; 432–426–3224).

In 1867, Forts Concho, Griffin, and Richardson were established and were occupied by the African American 10th Cavalry. Fort Concho, located in San Angelo is open daily (admission fee; located at 630 S. Oakes Street, San Angelo, TX 76903; 325–481–2646). Fort Griffin State Historic Site is also open daily (8:00 a.m. to 4:30 p.m.; admission fee; located at 1701 N. US Highway 283 Albany, Texas 76430; 325-762-3592). Fort Richardson State Park and Historic Site is also open daily (admission fee; located at 228 State Park Road 61, Jacksboro, Texas, 76458; 940-567-3506). To learn more about these and other frontier military posts, explore the Texas Forts Trail Region (http://texasfortstrail.com; 512-463-6100).

Camp Ford

Established in August 1863, Camp Ford was the largest Confederate Prisoner of War camp west of the Mississippi River. At its peak in July 1864, more than 5,300 Union soldiers were imprisoned here. It closed May 19, 1865, six days after the Battle of Palmito Ranch and two weeks before the surrender by Gen. E. Kirby Smith of the Trans-Mississippi Department of the Confederate States of America.

The site of Camp Ford (6500 US-271, Tyler, TX 75708; 903-592-5993) is now a public park managed by the Smith County Historical Society of Tyler, Texas (http://smithcountyhistoricalsociety.org/camp-ford/; see Alexander and Utley 2012: 72-77). The museum is open Tuesday through Saturday.

Battle Sites
Galveston

During the course of the Civil War, Galveston and its surroundings changed hands four times. From April 1861 to September 1862, it was a Confederate port. During the last four months of 1862, Union forces occupied the community. The Confederates retook the city in January 1863 and, although blockaded by the Union navy, held it to the end of the war. It was defended by no fewer than eleven small forts or batteries, specifically Fort Green, Fort Jackson, Fort Herbert, Fort Crockett, Fort Point, Fort Bankhead, Fort Magruder, Fort Moore, Fort Scurry, South Battery, and Redoubts Nos. 1, 2, and 3 (Texas Historic Sites Atlas http://www.northamericanforts.com/West/tx-coast1.html; see Alexander and Utley 2012: 66-71). One of the most successful Confederate blockade runners of the Civil War, the *Denbigh*, made five successful trips into Galveston during 1864 and 1865. It was destroyed there, on May 24, 1865, nine days before the surrender of the region by Gen. E. Kirby Smith. The ship was discovered in 1998, and is being studied by the Institute for Nautical Archaeology at Texas A&M University.

Sabine Pass

The Sabine Pass Battleground State Historic Site (open daily 9:00 a.m. to 5:00 p.m., free) is located fifteen miles south of Port Arthur on Highway 87. Here the September 8, 1863, defeat of a US Navy invasion force by Confederate forces known as the "Davis Guards" under the command of Lt. Richard Dowling at Fort Griffin is commemorated (Alexander and Utley 2012: 78–84).

Confederate Reunion Grounds

Limestone County near Mexia (FM 1633, Mexia, TX 76667) is the location of the Confederate Reunion Grounds State Historic Site. Open daily from 8:00 a.m. to 5:00 p.m. (admission fee; 254-472-0959), the Confederate Reunion Grounds was, from 1889–1946, a meeting place for Confederate veterans and their families. Here the veterans reaffirmed their Southern identity and created the Lost Cause Movement, which honored the Confederacy and raised funds for families of their fallen comrades. This is an important site for those wishing to understand the continued significance of the American Civil War in the South.

Mexico

Maximilian and the US Civil War

One cannot understand the significance of the Rio Grande in the American Civil War without recognizing it as an international boundary and thus not subject to naval blockade without that action being construed as an act of war. In the 1860s, the government of President Benito Juárez was friendly to the United States. He was deposed by Conservative factions with the backing of Napoleon III of France, who created a new North American empire under the rule of Ferdinand Maximilian Joseph von Habsburg. This new regime was friendly to the Confederacy.

Mexico from 1846 to 1876

During this thirty-year period, the great struggle between Conservatives and Liberals dominated the life of the Mexican nation. That struggle resulted in multiple wars. Conservatives believed that leadership of government should be restricted to an educated few and advocated limited suffrage, civil liberties, social services, a strong central government, and a state religion to guard the country's moral fiber. By contrast, Mexican Liberals advocated universal male suffrage, wide civil liberties, a weak and decentralized national government, and religious freedom. Following the loss of half of the nation's territory to the United States in 1848, Mexicans fought three civil wars. The first, from 1853 to 1855, ended with the overthrow of the Conservative government of Gen. Antonio Lopez de Santa Anna by Liberal forces under Juan Alvarez and Benito Juárez. The second conflict, known as the War of the Reform from 1857 to 1860, was a failed Conservative effort to overthrow the Juárez government and the Liberal Constitution of 1857. The third conflict, the War of the French Intervention from 1862 to 1867, saw French and Austrian forces invading Mexico and joining with Mexican Conservatives to reverse the outcome of the War of the Reform.

Rio Grande Valley Civil War Trail Mobil Web: 956-847-3002; Extension: 2956

Benito Juárez

For many Mexican citizens, Benito Juárez remains the most highly regarded of presidents, and to this day is the only Mexican president honored with the title of *Benémerito de las Americas* (Hero of the Americas). By heritage, a Zapotec Indian, Juárez was born in 1806. He received a basic seminary education and later graduated with a law degree from the Oaxacan Institute of Sciences and Arts. Juárez became known as an educator, lawyer, and member of the Oaxacan state legislature. After being elected to the national Chamber of Deputies, he emerged as a prominent Liberal leader, helping draft the Constitution of 1857, which extended rights to Mexican people. One provision of that charter, known as the *Ley Juárez*, abolished the legal privileges of the Church and the military. When Conservatives initiated a civil war aimed at annulling this constitution, Juárez led the Liberal forces to victory in the ensuing War of the Reform (1857-60). When the subsequent French invasion reached Mexico City, he refused to surrender and instead retreated to the north of México. Juárez and Abraham Lincoln shared much in common, sympathizing with each other's cause during the civil wars faced by their respective nations. Today Juárez-Lincoln High School in La Joya, Texas, commemorates these two great leaders. After the defeat of the French and the execution of Maximilian, Juárez resumed his duties as president in 1867. He was reelected to that post and served until his death in 1872 (see fig. 1.8).

Rio Grande Valley Civil War Trail Mobil Web: 956-847-3002; Extension: 2952

The Franco-Austrian Invasion

Mexican Conservatives would not accept their defeat in the War of the Reform in 1857. They remained convinced that Mexico should best be governed by an authoritarian monarch and sought a European aristocrat for that role. They settled on Emperor Napoleon III of France (irreverently known as Napoleon le Petite), who tried to expand France's overseas possessions and influence. Motivated by power and profit, Napoleon III had cultural reasons as well, viewing France as the natural leader of the Latin nations, which he considered superior to English-speaking nations. Napoleon III waited to make his move until the outbreak of the US Civil War, when Lincoln's government was preoccupied with the Confederacy. In 1862, France landed an army at Veracruz and began a march toward Mexico City. On May 5, 1862, his forces were defeated by the Mexican Army at the famous Battle of Puebla. This victory is now celebrated as Cinco de Mayo. The French, chastised by their defeat, increased the size of their forces and succeeded in capturing Mexico City a year later. There, they presided over the installation of Maximilian, Archduke of Austria, as emperor of Mexico. Benito Juárez's government fled north to the city that now bears his name, Ciudad Juárez. French forces pursued Juárez and his supporters into the north of the country, and in 1864, that pursuit brought them to the Rio Grande Valley.

Rio Grande Valley Civil War Trail Mobil Web: 956-847-3002; Extension: 2959

Mexico and the US Civil War

While the Union and Confederacy fought from 1861 to 1865, the supporters of Benito Juárez, known as *Juáristas*, fought the French and Austrian Imperialists from 1862 to 1867. The Rio Grande Valley became important in these struggles for several reasons. The US blockade of Confederate ports limited the South's ability to ship cotton and consequently limited the South's ability to import cannons, medical supplies, and other needed war materials. To circumvent the US Navy, Confederates utilized the small Mexican port of Bagdad, a place the Union could not attack without risking a war with France. Bagdad soon emerged as the Confederacy's major remaining port. To end this trade, the Union landed forces at Brazos de Santiago, marched inland to Brownsville, and subsequently headed northwest along the north bank of the river. The Confederates responded by moving the crossing points westward

Figure 8.6. Street scene on Calle de Cesar in Matamoros, Mexico. Courtesy of *Frank Leslie's Illustrated Newspaper*, February 20, 1864.

and later drove Union forces back to Brazos de Santiago. The tax revenue generated by the trade at Bagdad provided substantial revenue for the Mexican government. Although the Liberal commander of that part of Mexico, Juan Cortina, favored the Union, he could cooperate with both Northern and Southern forces as needed. When Matamoros briefly passed into the Imperialists' hands, the French and the Confederates cooperated as well. Although numerous hostile actions occurred on both sides of the river, no international war ever erupted between the Americans and Mexicans.

Rio Grande Valley Civil War Trail Mobil Web: 956-847-3002; Extension: 2957

Porfirio Diaz

Porfirio Diaz remains one of the most despised and enigmatic figures in Mexican history. Born in the state of Oaxaca and later a pupil of Benito Juárez, Diaz distinguished himself as a soldier in the Liberal armies. Already a general during the War of the French Intervention, he became nationally famous after leading the charge that routed the French at Puebla. But following two unsuccessful presidential campaigns, Diaz abandoned Liberalism and worked to overthrow the Mexican government. He began with an 1875 visit to New York City to enlist the support of US investors who wanted greater access to investment opportunities in Mexico. Diaz then proceeded to South Texas, where he raised several hundred thousand dollars from private supporters, including James Stillman, son of Charles Stillman, to train a small army. With this army, Diaz crossed the river and took Matamoros with little resistance on April 1, 1876. From then until 1910, a period known as the *Porfiriato*, Diaz ruled México with an iron fist. Although he took pride in the massive construction of railroads, including one from Matamoros to Monterrey (which was built by a group of investors led by James Stillman), and the development of mines, that growth was achieved at a fearsome cost. Diaz suppressed the civil liberties guaranteed in the Constitution of 1857, and evicted literally millions of Mexicans from their lands and homes to make way for commercial developments. By 1910, most Mexican citizens were poorer than they had been forty years earlier. This paved the way for the Mexican Revolution of 1910.

While in Brownsville, Diaz lived at the home of Manuel Trevino de los Santos Coy, Mexican Consul to Brownsville. This structure was formerly owned by Charles Stillman and is part of the Rio Grande Valley Civil War Trail. Visitors to the Stillman House will find exhibits relating to Porfirio Diaz and the Mexican Revolution.

Figure 8.7. Porfirio Diaz. Library of Congress Prints and Photographs Division, Washington, DC. Call Number Lot 3112, no. 88 [P&P]

Rio Grande Valley Civil War Trail Mobil Web: 956-847-3002; Extension: 2958

Matamoros (Also Known as Izucar de Matamoros and Heroica Ciudad de Matamoros)

The city of Matamoros, home to some 490,000 people, lies on the south bank of the Rio Grande, twenty miles from the Gulf of Mexico. The community was founded in 1774 by José de Escandón, who issued land grants to 113 families. Because of its proximity to the fertile lands along the Rio Grande and northeastern Mexico, Matamoros grew steadily. By the late 1850s, about forty thousand people lived there. Among its residents were Mexicans with substantial land holdings, as well as several hundred Anglo merchants. These included Mifflin Kenedy, Richard King, and Charles Stillman, men who shaped the history of the river's north bank. In the 1850s, the enormous commerce generated after the establishment of a free trade zone, and the presence of nearby Bagdad as a port sympathetic to the Confederate cause, allowed Matamoros to prosper until the end of the US Civil War. John Warren Hunter, who transported cotton to Matamoros, described it as a "great commercial center" filled with "ox trains, mule trains, and trains of Mexican carts, all laden with cotton coming from almost every town in Texas."[1] In 1864 and 1865, Gen. Tomas Mejia at the head of a combined Austrian, Belgian, French, and Mexican army occupied Matamoros and the southern banks of the Rio Grande. Friendly to the Confederate cause, these soldiers were said to regularly frequent Brownsville. In fact, during the May 1865 battle of Palmito Ranch, these troops provided intelligence to the Confederates of the movement of Union forces. With the end of the American Civil War, many former Confederates made their way to Mexico to serve in the army of Maximilian. The border was anything but peaceful, as there were repeated clashes between the armies of Imperial Mexico and the United States, including the occupation of Bagdad in January 1866 by US forces and the shelling of Brownsville by a French gunboat. On June 18, 1866, following his defeat at the battle of Santa Gertrudis near Camargo, Tamaulipas, Gen. Mejia evacuated the region. With peace, the town's population declined rapidly after the Civil War ended. By 1880, Matamoros's economy had stagnated, with barely eight thousand people remaining.

1. http://www.utrgv.edu/civilwar-trail/civil-war-trail/imperial-mexico/matamoros/index.htm. Accessed December 5, 2017.

Figure 8.8. Juan Nepomuceno Cortina defeating Don Manuel Ruiz and the Matamoros militia, as depicted by *Frank Leslie's Illustrated Newspaper*, February 20, 1864. Although Cortina and Ruiz were allies prior to this conflict, Cortina assumed the role of governor and military leader of Tamaulipas as a result of this victory.

Figure 8.9. Juan Nepomuceno Cortina defeated pro-US Liberal military governor of Tamaulipas, Don Manuel Ruiz, in Matamoros, as depicted by *Frank Leslie's Illustrated Newspaper*, February 20, 1864. After this victory, Cortina was eventually promoted to the rank of general by the Central Mexican government, and proceeded to negotiate with both Confederate and Union forces to his benefit, as it pertained to cross-border trade.

TEXAS HISTORIC COMMISSION—MARKER #275
BAGDAD-MATAMOROS, C.S.A.

Civil War "Sister Cities," across the river in neutral Mexico. Were linked to Texas by a ferry which landed here. Ferry hauled to Matamoros the Confederate cotton brought from East Texas, Louisiana, Arkansas to Brownsville. In Matamoros, many speculators and agents vied for cotton to ship to Europe, via Havana. They offered in exchange vital goods: guns, ammunition, drugs, shoes, cloth. At Bagdad, on the Gulf, cotton was loaded from small boats onto ships riding the Gulf of Mexico. Goods crossing here were the South's lifeblood.

Location: South of the Rio Grande in Mexico
GPS Coordinates: Latitude 25° 56′ 37.86″ N Longitude 97° 08′ 53.46″ W
Access: None
Rio Grande Valley Civil War Trail Mobile Web: 956–847–3002; **Extensions:** 2001 and 2955

Further Reading

Alexander, Thomas E., and Dan K. Utley. *Faded Glory: A Century of Forgotten Military Sites in Texas, Then and Now*. A Texas A&M Travel Guide edition. College Station: Texas A&M University Press, 2012.

Levinson, Irving W. "Separate Wars and Shared Destiny: México and the United States from 1861 to 1878." Chapter 5 in *The Civil War on the Rio Grande, 1846–1876*, edited by Roseann Bacha-Garza, Christopher L. Miller, and Russell K. Skowronek. College Station: Texas A&M University Press, 2019.

Epilogue

*Now this is not the end. It is not even the beginning of the end.
But it is, perhaps, the end of the beginning.*
—*Winston Churchill*

It is hard to imagine that it was only at the beginning of January 2011, days before the opening of the Society for Historical Archaeology meeting in Austin titled, "Boundaries and Crossroads in Action: Global Perspectives in Historical Archaeology," that Dr. W. Stephan McBride stated, "Fort Ringgold was the best preserved nineteenth century U.S. Army installation in the country, and no one knows about it." Four years later in 2015, not only Fort Ringgold but a two hundred mile long section of the Rio Grande was immortalized with the launch of the Rio Grande Valley Civil War Trail. This was the seminal moment in what now can be recognized as the birth of a regional approach to heritage tourism.

This current undertaking is built on the work underlying Los Caminos del Rio, an earlier generation's effort to identify historic sites in both Mexico and the United States from the Gulf of Mexico to Laredo, and the "Texas Tropical Trail." Built on traditional printed materials, today's efforts melds ongoing research, K–12 education, community lectures, the Internet, social media, and other on air media with an eye toward marketing the trail to local families, educators, "spring breakers," winter Texans, and eco-tourists who either call the Rio Grande region home or make it a destination.

This book serves as a companion to the trail guide/map and associated web page, and as an overview for the in-depth Texas A&M University Press book, *The Civil War on the Rio Grande, 1846-1876* (2019). The trail and associated scholarship and tourism opportunities will evolve in coming years. Someday it may extend to Del Rio or may follow the Gulf coast of Texas to include other Civil War era sites as far as the Sabine River. Along the Rio Grande, it will be joined by other "trails" that will celebrate the region's rich natural history and broader cultural history. The dream of a heritage corridor, as expressed by the creators of Los Caminos del Rio, is only limited by the imagination of those who follow. Someday there will be hiking and biking trails and interpretive exhibits that will continue to enhance the visitor experience.

Thank you for taking this journey with us. In the meantime, please look out for signs marking the route of the Rio Grande Valley Civil War Trail. We look forward to seeing you.

Figure E.1. Rio Grande Valley Civil War Trail highway sign that appears along the two hundred mile trail between Brownsville and Laredo. This sign is located near the entrance to Palmito Ranch Battlefield on Highway 4 in Brownsville. Thanks to a grant from the Brownsville Community Improvement Corporation, there are multiple locations throughout Cameron County that help mark the trail. The Zapata County Historical Museum has also sponsored a sign.

To learn more about the Rio Grande Valley Civil War Trail:

Figure E.2. Scan this image from your smart device to visit the Rio Grande Valley Civil War Trail website to view the entire virtual trail and experience the multi-media content associated with it.

Figure E.3. Scan this image from your smart device to visit the Palo Alto Battlefield National Historical Park's four mobile web tours: Taylor's Trail (US-Mexican War), the Rio Grande Valley Civil War Trail, a Battlefield Safari, and the Fort Brown Historical Tour (created by the CHAPS Program in 2018).

About the Authors

Roseann Bacha-Garza (MA, University of Texas–Pan American) is the program manager of the Community Historical Archaeology Project with Schools (CHAPS) Program at the University of Texas Rio Grande Valley in Edinburg, Texas. Outlined in her thesis, "San Juan and Its Role in the Transformation of the Rio Grande Valley," is the succession of Spanish land grantees, displaced Civil War families, Anglo entrepreneurs, and Mexican Revolution refugees and their migration to San Juan at various stages of municipal development. She coedited several books, including *The Civil War on the Rio Grande, 1846–1876* (with Russell Skowronek and Christopher Miller, 2019), *The Native American Peoples of South Texas* (2014), and *From Porciones to Colonias: The Power of Place and Community-Based Learning in K–12 Education* (2014). She wrote *Images of America: San Juan* (2010), in collaboration with the San Juan Economic Development Corporation, which won Preservation Texas' Heritage Education Award.

Born and raised in Portland, Oregon, **Christopher L. Miller** received his bachelor of science degree from Lewis and Clark College and his PhD from the University of California, Santa Barbara. He is currently professor of history at the University of Texas Rio Grande Valley. He is the author of *Prophetic Worlds: Indians and Whites on the Columbia Plateau* (1985); coauthor of *Making America: A History of the United States*, now in its seventh edition (2015); and coeditor with Tamer Balcı of *The Gülen Hizmet Movement: Circumspect Activism in Faith-Based Reform* (2012). His articles and reviews have appeared in numerous scholarly journals and anthologies as well as standard reference works. He has been a research fellow at the Charles Warren

Center for Studies in American History at Harvard University, was the Nikolay V. Sivachev Distinguished Chair in American History at Lomonsov Moscow State University (Russia), and is the codirector of the CHAPS Program, where he helped facilitate the Rio Grande Valley Civil War Trail and also coedited, with Roseann Bacha-Garza and Russell K. Skowronek, *The Civil War on the Rio Grande, 1846–1876* (2019).

Russell K. Skowronek (PhD, Michigan State University), the Houston Endowment Chair for Civic Engagement and a research associate of the Smithsonian Institution, is Associate Dean for the School of Interdisciplinary Programs and Community Engagement in the College of Liberal Arts, and professor of anthropology and history at the University of Texas Rio Grande Valley. There he serves as the director of the CHAPS Program. He is the author or editor of several books, including *The Civil War on the Rio Grande, 1846–1876* (with Roseann Bacha-Garza and Christopher Miller, 2019), *X Marks the Spot: The Archaeology of Piracy* (with Charles R. Ewen, 2006), *Situating Mission Santa Clara de Asís* (2006), *HMS Fowey Lost...and Found* (with George Fischer, 2009), *Beneath the Ivory Tower: The Archaeology of Academia* (with Kenneth Lewis, 2010), *Recovering a Legacy: The Ceramics of Alta California* (with M. James Blackman and Ronald L. Bishop, 2014), and *Pieces of Eight: More Archaeology of Piracy* (with Charles R. Ewen, 2016).

Index

Page numbers in *italics* refer to figures and tables.

abolition. *See* Emancipation Proclamation; slavery
Adams, John Quincy, 8
African American Union forces. *See* US Colored Troops
Albuerne, Juan Rodríguez de, 4
American Civil War. *See* US Civil War
Anaconda Plan, 17. *See also* Lincoln, Abraham
Appomattox Courthouse, 22, 60
Arista, Mariano, 34, 65

Bagdad, Mexico, 18, 19, 26, 44, 45, 69–71, *71, 72, 73, 75*, 182
Banks, Nathaniel P., 19, 21, 50, 59
Barrera y Garza, Tomás Sánchez de la, 6
Barrett, Theodore H., 23–24, 60–62
Battle of El Clareño. *See* El Clareño
Battle of La Bolsa Bend. *See* La Bolsa Bend, battle of
Battle of Palmito Ranch. *See* Palmito Ranch, battle of
Battle of Palo Alto. *See* Palo Alto, battle of
Battle of Puebla. *See* Puebla, battle of
Battle of Resaca de la Palma. *See* Resaca de la Palma, battle of
Battle of San Jacinto. *See* San Jacinto, battle of
Bee, Hamilton Prioleau, 19, *19*, 20, 50, *57*
Benavides, Basilio, 6
Benavides, Cristobal, 21
Benavides, Santos, biography, 150–54; El Clareño massacre, 135–36; grave site, *153*; home, *147*; in Laredo, 21; photo, *15*; political career, 28, 151; at Rancho Davis, 109; at Redmond's Ranch, 137, 138; Zapata County conflicts: 14–15
Benavides family, 6, *146*, 150–54, *152, 153*
blockades, 17, 19, 21, 48, 182
Boca Chica Beach. *See* Sheridan's Bridge
Branson, David, 23, 60
Brazos Island, 19, *22*, 22–24, 44–46, 56, 73, 81, 163, *169–70*, 171, 182
Brazos Santiago. *See* Brazos Island
Brown, Jacob, 9, 38, 64
Brownsville, 48–51; and the Civil War, 18–24; ferry trade, *49*; founding of, 11; Hebrew Cemetery, 54; Heritage Museum, *56*; Levee Street, *164*; Market Square, *49*; Old City Cemetery, 33, 51–54; *52, 53*; Palo Alto Battlefield National Historic Park, 33, 35–36, *35*, 40, 191; Stillman House, 33, 55–57, *55*; William A. Neale House, 57–58, *58*
Buell, Don Carlos, 41
Buffalo Soldiers, 27, 109; national museum, 2, 167–68, *168*. *See also* US Colored Troops

Calhoun, John C., 8
Camargo, 5, 79, 103, 104, 124, 185
Cameron County, 32–77; map of, *32*; Mexican-American War in, 34–39; US Civil War in, 40–77
Camp Ford, 179
Camp Nelson, 167; Civil War Heritage Park, 167

Camp Ringgold. *See* Ringgold Barracks
Canby, Edward R. S., 24
Carrizo confrontation, 134–35
Chapa, Jose Florencio de, 103
Cinco de Mayo, 17, 182
Clareño massacre. *See* Rancho Clareño
Clarksville, Texas, 71–73, *73*, 170
Clay Davis, Henry, 104
Clearwater, Theresa Clark, 72
Coahuila y Tejas, 6–7, 79
Confederate Army. *See* US Civil War
Confederate Reunion Grounds, 180
Conservatives. *See* Mexican Conservatives
Cortés, Hernán, 3
Cortina, Juan Nepomuceno: Cortina War, 107–8; defeat, 107; as governor of Tamaulipas, 26; guerilla army, 11–12; at La Bolsa Bend, 96–97; in Matamoros, *186*; photo, *11*; at Redmond's Ranch, 14–15, 137; retirement, 28; Union/Confederate allegiance, 183
Cortina, María Estéfana Goseascochea de, 11
Cortina War. *See* Cortina, Juan Nepomuceno; La Bolsa Bend, battle of
Cortinistas, 11–12, 97, 137. *See also* Cortina, Juan Nepomuceno
Costilla, Miguel Hidalgo y, 80
cotton trade, 17–18, 21, 48–50, 87–88; at Bagdad, 69; at Clarksville, 71; at Fort Brown, 64, 85; at Roma, 120–22; on the Rio Grande, *18*, 118, 123; trade routes, *20*; Union blockades, 17, 19, 21, 48, 182
Cox, Noah, 124–25

Dana, Napoleon, 44, 64
Davis, Edmund J., 139–40
Davis, Henry Clay, 105
Davis Landing. *See* Ringgold Barracks
Diaz, Porfirio, biography, 183–85; Mexican liberation, 26; photo, *184*; and Juan Nepomuceno Cortina, 28
Dolores, 5, 6, 131
Duff, James, 19
Duncan, James, 10
Dye, William, 19

Eagle Pass, 21
Edinburgh. *See* Hidalgo (city of)

El Clareño, 135–36, *136*, *138*; massacre at, 135–36
El Desierto Muerto, 6–7
El Fronton. *See* Point Isabel
Eli Jackson Cemetery. *See* Jackson Ranch
Emancipation Proclamation, 162, 166–67. *See also* slavery
Emperor Maximilian: colonies, 24; fall of, 81; at Palmito Ranch 62; photo, *16*; Querétaro siege, 26; rise to power, 17; in the US Civil War, 180
Escandón, José de: in Laredo, 143, 145; in Matamoros, 185; in Nuevo Santander, 86, 103, 106; in Old Zapata, 133; sculpture of, *4*; and Spanish colonization, 4–5. *See also* Nuevo Santander
Escobedo, Mariano, 26

Flores, Cesáreo, 139, *139*. *See also* Zapata County
Ford, John Salmon "Rip": at Fort Brown, 65; at La Bolsa Bend, 97; at Las Rucias, 58–59; military career, 14–15, 21–22; at Palmito Ranch, 62, 64; photo, *12*, *110*; political career, 13, 28; at Ringgold Barracks, 109; secession, 13
Fort Brown, 9, 22, 36–38, 64–69; blueprints, *9*, *37*; Confederate officers at, 42; construction, 36–38; commissary, *70*; Cavalry barracks, *69*; guardhouse, *70*; earthworks, *37*, *38*; morgue, *68*; post hospital, *25*, *67*; Texas Southmost College campus, 25, 65–69, *67*, *68*, *69*, *70*; Union officers at, 41
Fort Duncan, 9–10
Fort McIntosh, 9, 14, 26, 156–61; barracks, *161*; bakery, *158*; guardhouse, *160*, *171*; hospital, *159*; officer's quarters, *159*, *160*; storehouse, *158*; maps of *157*, *158*
Fort Polk. *See* Point Isabel
Fort Ringgold. *See* Ringgold Barracks
Fort Sumter, surrender of, 14
Fort Texas. *See* Fort Brown
Fort Treviño, 132. *See also* San Ygnacio
Fort Worth. *See* Texas Civil War Museum
Franco-Austrian Invasion, 182

Galveston, 179
Garza Falcón, Blas María de la, 11, 103

General Order No. 3, 24. *See also* Emancipation Proclamation; slavery
Granger, General Gordon, 24
Grant, Ulysses S., 22, 41, 166

Halleck, Henry, 19
Havana, Texas, 88–90
Hebrew Cemetery. *See* Brownsville
Herron, Francis J., 22, 46
Hicks, Matilda, 91
Hidalgo (city of), 87–88, *87*
Hidalgo County, 78–100; Havana, 88–90; interracial marriage in, 80, 91–92; Jackson Ranch, 91–93; La Bolsa, 96–98; La Sal del Rey, 83–85; map of, *78*; McAllen Ranch, 85–86; Museum of South Texas History, 81–82; Peñitas Cemetery, 90–91; Relámpago Ranch, 95–96; salt lakes, 82–85; Veteran's War Memorial of Texas, 98–100; Webber's Ranch, 93–95. *See also* Hidalgo (city of)
Hinojosa, Lino, 118–19, *119*
Hord, Edward R., 125
Houston, Sam, 8, 13

Imperial Army, 25–26

Jackson, Nathaniel, 91–92. *See also* Jackson Ranch
Jackson Ranch, 91–93; church, *92*; Eli Jackson Cemetery, 93
John Vale/Noah Cox House, 124–25
Juan Cortina Battle, 107–8
Juárez, Benito: biography, 181; vs. Conservative government, 181; vs. the Imperial Army, 25–26; Liberal government, 16; and Lincoln, 81; photo, *16*; Union alliance, 81, 180. *See also* Mexican Liberals; Juáristas
Juáristas, 17, 18, 26
Juneteenth, 24

Kenedy, Mifflin, 10, 12, 19, 28, 55 107, 117, 178. 185
King Ranch, 174–76, *175*
King, Richard: as anti-Cortina, 12, 107; as a capitalist, 10, 19, 28, 117; King Ranch, 174–76, photo, *175*; as a Union ally, 55. *See also* Mifflin Kenedy Warehouse; King Ranch
Kleiber, Joseph, 125

La Bolsa Bend, battle of, 12, *96*, 96–98
La Habitación. *See* Hidalgo (city of)
La Sal del Rey, 21, *83*, 83–85
La Salle, René-Robert Cavelier, Sieur de, 3–4
La Soledad, 137–38
Lara, Bernardo Gutiérrez de, 134
Laredo, 5, 7, 9, 21, 104, 140, 143–61
Laredo Community College. *See* Fort McIntosh
Las Rucias, 21, *59*, 59–60
Lee, Robert E.: at Ringgold Barracks, 12, 115–17; surrender, 22, 62, 163. *See also* Robert E. Lee house
Leyendecker, John Z., 145, *146*, *147*
Liberals. *See* Mexican Liberals
Lincoln, Abraham: and abolition, 162; and Benito Juárez, 81, 181; blockades, 17; Brownsville attack, 19; election, 13; formation of the US Colored Troops, 162–63; General Order No. 3, 162–63. *See also* Emancipation Proclamation
Longstreet, James, 41
Los Saenz Cemetery, 118, *120*
Lost Cause Movement, 180
Lower Rio Grande Valley. *See* Rio Grande Valley
Loya, José María, 90, *91*

Maltby, Henry A., 18
Matamoros, 5, *6*, 34, 183, 184, 185–87
Maximilian of Habsburg. *See* Emperor Maximilian
McAllen, John, 10, *10*, 80, 85
McAllen Ranch, 85–86
McIntosh, James S., 9
Meade, George Gordon, 41
Mejia, Tomas, 185
Mexican Conservatives, 7, 16, 181
Mexican Liberals, 16, 180
Mexican Revolution, 184, 193
Mexican War, 7–13, 34–39; annexation of Texas, 8, 34; beginning of, 38–39; Brownsville militia, 11–12; end of, 26, 80; guerrilla presence in, 11–12; regional battles, *36*; and slavery, 8; Texas Rangers in, 12
Mexican-American War. *See* Mexican War
Mexico Bay. *See* Seno Mexicano
Mier, 5, 33, 79, 103, 103, 104, 133, 138

Index 197

Mifflin Kenedy Warehouse, 117–18
Military Highway, 39, 60, 87, 88, 92, 93, 94, 97
mining, 5, 84
Murrah, Pendleton, 24
Museum of South Texas History, 81–82. *See also* Hidalgo

Napoleon III, 16, 25, 81, 180
Native American influence: Indian Wars, 27; nomadic harvesting, 3; raids, 24, 115, 143, 165; salt mining, 83, 104
Neale, William A., 57–58
Neale House. *See* Brownsville
New Spain, 79, 90
Nueces River, 6–7, 34, 79
Nuevo Santander, 5, 7, 86, 103, 143, 145, 147

Ochoa, Antonio, 14–15, 134, 135
Old City Cemetery. *See* Brownsville
Old Rio Grande City Cemetery, 118–20

Palmito Ranch, battle of, 23, 60–64, *61, 62, 63,* 165–66, 179, 185
Palo Alto, battle of, 9, 35, 40–43; Confederate officers at, 42; Union officers at, 41, 43
Palo Alto Battlefield National History Park, 33, 35–36, *35,* 40, 191. *See also* Brownsville
Pemberton, John, 41
Peñitas Cemetery, 90–91, *91*
Pérez, Patricio, 80, 89–90, *89*
Pettibone, Augustus, 43
Planque, Louis de, 18
Point Isabel, 73–77. *See also* Port Isabel
Polk, James K., 8, 34, 75
Port Isabel, 35, 57, 72, 73–77; Historical Museum, 33, 74, *75*; Light Station / Lighthouse, *76*
Puebla, battle of, 17

Ramirez, Mario, 126. *See also* Roma (city of)
Ramirez House / Ramirez Memorial Hospital, 125–26
Ramirez Memorial Hospital, 125–26
Rancho Clareño massacre, 14
Rancho de Carricitos, 38–39; *39*

Rancho San Luis. *See* Hidalgo (city of)
Rancho Santa Anita. *See* McAllen Ranch
Reconstruction, 23–28, 139–40. *See also* US Civil War
Redmond, Henry, 14
Redmond, John, 137
Redmond's Ranch, 15, 137
Refugio (villa of), 5
Reinosa. *See* Reynosa
Relámpago Ranch, 95–96
Republic of Texas, 7–8, 33–34, 79
Resaca de la Palma, battle of, 9, 39–40, *40*
Revilla, 5, 6, 132, 133
Reynosa, 5, 79, 86, 87
Rhodes, Thaddeus, 95. *See also* Relámpago Ranch
Ringgold, Samuel, 108–9
Ringgold Barracks, xiii, 12, 26, 104–5, 108–15, *109, 112*; hospital, *111*; officer's quarters, *113*; morgue, *114*; Robert E. Lee House, *116*; stables, *114*
Rio Grande, as a border, 9; as a trade route, 103
Rio Grande City, 21, 105–7, *105*; Mifflin Kenedy Warehouse, 117–18; Old Rio Grande City Cemetery, 118–20
Rio Grande Valley: colonization of, 3–8; mercantiles in, 5; Mexican rule in, 7–8; mining in, 5; and Indian raids, 6; ranching in, 5; Spanish influence in, 4–7
Rio Grande Valley Civil War Trail: creation of, xii–xix; Contributors Committee, *xx*; future directions, xviii–xix; ribbon cutting ceremony, xvii; road signs, *190*; website, xvii, 191
Robert E. Lee house, 115–17. *See also* Lee, Robert E.
Roma (city of): historic district, 120–23; John Vale/Noah Cox House, 124–25; *125*; Ramirez House/Ramirez Memorial Hospital, 125–26, *126*; Roma Plaza, *123*; Union blockades, 21; World Birding Visitor's Center, *121*
Roma Historic District, 120–23
Ruiz, Don Manuel, *186*

Sabine Pass, 180
Sal del Rey. *See* La Sal del Rey
salt mining, 5, 82–84, 104
San Bartolo, 14–15, 137

San Jacinto, battle of, 7–8
San Luisito. *See* Hidalgo (city of)
San Yganacio, 32, 131–34
Santa Anna, Antonio Lopez de, 7, 181
Santa Gertrudis/Cervalo, battle of, 26
Santa Gertrudis Ranch. *See* King Ranch
Scott, Winfield, 17
Second Battle of El Clareño. *See* El Clareño
Sedgwick, Thomas, 26
Seno Mexicano, 3, 4, 6
Sheridan, Philip, 46
Sheridan's Bridge, 46–48, *47*, *48*
Slaughter, James E., 24, 62, 74, 87, *87*, 156
slavery: abolition, 24, 162, 166–67; and the Civil War, 162; escape across the Mexican border, 10, 81, 92; General Order No. 3, 24; and interracial marriage, 80, 91–92, 94
Slidell, John, 8
Smith, Edmund Kirby, 24, 41, 179
Soledad, Confederate attack at, 16–17, 137–38
Spanish settlement of the Rio Grande, 3–8; mercantiles, 5; ranching, 5; salt mining, 5, 82–84, 104; Vera Cruz invasion, 16. *See also* Camargo; Dolores; Laredo; Mier; New Spain; Nuevo Santander; Revilla; Reynosa
St. Augustine Plaza, 21, 145–50, *148*, *149*
Starr, James Harper, 105
Starr County, 101–26; John Vale/Noah Cox House, 124–25; Juan Cortina battle, 107–8; map of, *101*; Mifflin Kenedy Warehouse, 117–18; Old Rio Grande City Cemetery, 118–20; Rio Grande City, 105–7; Ringgold Barracks, 108–15; Robert E. Lee house, 115–17; Ramirez House/Ramirez Memorial Hospital, 125–26; Roma Historic District, 120–23
Stillman, Charles, 10, 11, 19, 28, 55–58, 106, 185
Stillman House. *See* Brownsville

Tamaulipas, 5, 44
Tampico, 3
Taylor, Richard, 20
Taylor, Zachary, 34, *34*, 39, 44, 64, 124
Temple, Phillip, 21, 59

Texas Civil War Museum, 176–78, *176*, *177*
Texas Rangers, 11–12, 107
Texas Southmost College. *See* Fort Brown
Thornton Skirmish. *See* Rancho de Carricitos
Torrejón, Anastasio, 39
Treaty of Guadalupe Hidalgo, 9, 17, 80, 129
Treaty of Velasco, 7, 8
Treviño, Jesús, 6
Treviño Fort. *See* Fort Treviño
Twiggs, David, 64
Tyler, John, 8

Union Army. *See* US Civil War
Upshur, Abel P., 8
US Civil War, 3–28, 40–77; battle sites, 179–80; beginning of, 14, 134; Camp Ford, 179; Confederate Army officers, 42–43; and Emperor Maximilian, 180; end of, 22, 60–64; forts used, 178–79; French involvement in, 17; at King Ranch, 174–76; in Matamoros 185–87; Mexican involvement in, 180–85; Reconstruction, 23, 139–40; along the Rio Grande, 13–28; secession, 13–14; Texas Civil War Museum, 176–78; in Texas and Mexico, 174–87; Union Army officers, 41; Union blockades, 17, 19, 21, 48, 182; Union victory, 60–64
US Colored Infantry. *See* US Colored Troops
US Colored Troops, 23–27, 44, 46, 50, 60, 65, 72, 81, 162–73, 109; and Abraham Lincoln, 163; and Benito Juárez, 163; in Cameron County, 169–71; at Camp Nelson, 167; after the Civil War, 165; in Clarksville, 170; flag, *172*; at Fort Brown, 170; in Hidalgo County, 171–72; at Palmito Ranch, 165–66, 171; at Ringgold Barracks, 172; in Roma, 173; in Starr County, 172–73; in Webb County, 173; at White's Ranch, 171; in Zapata County, 173. *See also* Buffalo Soldiers
USCT. *See* US Colored Troops

Vale, John Henrik, 10, 19, 122, 123–25, *124*. *See also* Roma (city of)

Index 199

Vela, Isidro, 14–15, 134, 135, 138
Veteran's War Memorial of Texas,
   98–100, *98–99*
villas, 5–6

Wallace, Lewis, 23–24
Webb County, 143–61; Benavides
   brothers in, 150–54; Casa Ortiz, 150;
   Fort McIntosh, 156–61; map of, *142*;
   St. Augustine Plaza, 145–50; Zacate
   Creek, 154–55
Webber, John, 93–94. *See also* Webber's Ranch
Webber's Ranch, 93–95; cemetery, *94*
Wild Horse Desert. *See* El Desierto Muerto
Williams, John Jefferson, 23, *61*, 62, 64

Young, John, 10, 80, 85, 87

Zacate Creek, 21, 154–55, *155*
Zamora, Ignacio, 80, 90, *91*
Zapata, Antonio, 129
Zapata, Octaviano, 81, 137, 138
Zapata County, 128–61; Carrizo confrontation, 134–35; El Clareño, 135–36, 138–39; La Soledad, 137–38; map of, *128, 130*; pro-Unionism in, 14; Museum of History, *129*, 130; Reconstruction in, 139–40; Redmond's Ranch, 137; San Ygnacio, 131–34
Zaragoza, Ignacio, 17

LA SAL
DEL REY

186

HIDALGO
COUNTY

EDINBURG

McALLEN

83 2

77

281

MEXICO